WILL INFLATION DESTROY AMERICA?

Also by Arthur Milton

Life Insurance Stocks: The Modern Gold Rush
How to Get a Dollar's Value for a Dollar Spent
Insurance Stocks, a Fortune to Share
Inflation: Everyone's Problem
Something More Can Be Done!
Life Insurance Stocks: An Investment Appraisal
You Are Worth a Fortune

WILL INFLATION DESTROY AMERICA?

by Arthur Milton

The Citadel Press/Secaucus, N.J.

First edition

Published by Citadel Press
A division of Lyle Stuart Inc.
120 Enterprise Ave., Secaucus, N.J. 07094
In Canada: George J. McLeod Limited, Toronto
Typography by David E. Seham Associates
Manufactured in the United States of America

Library of Congress Cataloging in Publication Data

Milton, Arthur, 1922–
Will inflation destroy America?

1. Inflation (Finance)—United States. I. Title.
HG538.M653 332.4'1'0973 77-21629
ISBN 0-8065-0608-3

For her wit, companionship, intellect,
love, affection and constant understanding
I dedicate this book to Phyllis

CONTENTS

FOREWORD

On dune and headland sinks the fire
The captains and the kings depart.
Lo, our pomp of yesteryear
Is one with Nineveh and Tyre.
Lord God of Hosts, spare us yet,
Spare us yet. Lest we forget!

When Rudyard Kipling wrote these lines for Queen Victoria's jubilee nearly eighty years ago, he shocked England profoundly. Britain was at the zenith of her imperial power and Kipling was regarded as the most imperialist of poets.

That he could presume to remind Her Imperial Majesty, the Widow of Windsor, that the forces of dissolution were already at work in the empire on which the sun never set was incredible. Yet in only twenty years the empire not only had begun to crumble, but England itself was reduced to modest circumstances.

Today Britain lives in genteel poverty, with few remaining overseas possessions. The once-proud pound sterling is one of the world's less valued currencies. The Navy that ruled all the seas is no more. The merchant fleet and shipbuilding industry that at the start of the century were by far the greatest on earth, are today relatively unimportant. British banking, insurance and manufacturing likewise have withered.

We Americans speak English, although our forebears came here from every corner of the globe. Our concepts of government, law and freedom are derived from England, so we all are sensitive to Britain's fate; we have been allied with her in three wars in this century.

On rereading Kipling's somber reminder to Victoria, which he entitled *Recessional,* it strikes one with sudden, grim force that the ghost of Kipling could be speaking to us today. Kipling knew us well. He lived in the United States for some years and did some of his better writing here.

The pace of the world has accelerated considerably since we reached the zenith of our international power in 1945, and since about 1955 we have been frittering that power and strength away. We in the U.S.A. are still frittering it away because we lack the will to bring under control the unrestrained inflation that is wrecking our economy. Inflation is corrupting every level of our society and breeding cynicism, frustration, crime and despair among large elements of our populace.

Arthur Milton's book is an examination of all the major facets of inflation and a grim warning that if we don't bring unrestrained inflation to heel soon, our pomp of yesteryear also will be "one with the ancient city states of Nineveh and Tyre." The beloved Stars and Stripes might indeed be shrouded in the twilight's last gleaming, followed by an unending darkness.

FRANK ANGELL
Professor of Finance
New York University

INTRODUCTION

The disruption of industry and commerce during the bitter winter of 1976–77, sent inflation in the United States soaring to ten per cent a year, after it had dropped to the lowest level in four years.

Even the 1976 rate was about twice as great as what could safely be considered acceptable. As the nation neared midyear, the outlook was far from encouraging.

Uncontrolled inflation is a potent breeder of profiteering and numerous commercial rackets. It also causes a vast amount of political, business and professional corruption and crime of every kind. It simultaneously creates incentives for criminal acts and provides front or seed money to enable criminals and political terrorists to attempt audacious and violent offenses. These crimes would be much more difficult to plan and carry out in a more stable economic climate.

Many books and articles on inflation have appeared in recent years. I wrote one myself in 1968 entitled *Inflation: Everyone's Problem.* It was a brief historical account of galloping inflation in past centuries up to and through the inflation caused by the war in Vietnam, then at its peak. I spoke of Europe's vexed fear that a vast flood of eurodollars might soon cause uncontrolled inflation. The only antidote to inflation I proposed, was to advise people to work hard and save.

Many books on inflation were more ambitious. Some were academic textbooks advancing very abstruse ideas. Others were written in varying degrees of anger by business leaders who fervently believed that the substitution of collective bargaining power for the law of supply and demand in the labor market, is the one great cause of inflation. They argued for legal prohibition of national bargaining by unions. One earnest business man who has researched the subject thoroughly and lectured and written about it for years, advocated the creation of a type of corporate sub-government in the United States to control wage and price levels and prevent inflation.

Another businessman was convinced that all we have to do to eliminate inflation is do away with the drones in the population. He also urged the substitution of a system of direct legislation by the voters, through initiated referendums, for a large part of the present powers of Congress and the Supreme Court in order to deal with the causes of inflation.

But it seems to me that all this widespread preoccupation with the notion that the bargaining power of labor is the basic cause of uncontrolled inflation misses the mark. For one thing, government statistics show, that although the unions' bargaining power really is great enough to determine wage levels, the absolute proportion of union workers has not kept up with population growth, hence there are more non-union than union workers. Moreover, in spite of the investment power of their pension funds, the unions have little control over capital investment, so they cannot control productivity levels. When all is said and done, productivity is the vital element in the economy, not wage levels.

Many business leaders and economists who write about inflation recognize this and seek means to tie wage levels to productivity. It is amazing that so many persons are naive enough to believe human passions can be sufficiently repressed to make that possible. They simply ignore the lessons of history.

The record of civilization is the story of the struggle of the common man—the chained field hand and gang laborer, the physician, the teacher, the scribe and the soldier—up from chattel slavery, to rise from starvation and the lash and the cross, to some measure of self-respect and well being. For untold centuries man's struggle has been to take away a bigger share of the fruits of his own toil from his tyrannical and cruel masters. It is ridiculous to imagine that he ever will be content to accept the idea that he is worth only what his masters think he produces.

So, the more I look at the matter, the more I have concluded that while the rising standard of living of the workers inevitably causes a slow and perceptible rate of inflation, it has little or nothing to do with uncontrolled inflation. Uncontrolled inflation is still what it always has been—a reflex of war or of the fear of war, which produces the crushing burden of supporting huge armies and vast armaments.

There still remains the question of the individual's personal attitude towards productivity, inflation, and the corruption and crime that result from inflation. I have tried to deal with this by a fervent appeal to all Americans to return to our historic respect for the work ethic.

ARTHUR MILTON

1.

INFLATION BREEDS LAWLESSNESS

If the good life in America, a life affording opportunity and the hope of happiness to ordinary folk, is to be maintained, our most pressing task is to bring a permanent end to uncontrolled inflation.

It can be done.

If we don't do it by the year 2000, a bare twenty-two years hence, then the fruits of more than two centuries of toil, struggle, dreams and achievement on the part of our forebears will have been in vain. The mightiest and most splendid nation in the history of man will be blighted and destroyed. The most beautiful vision and freedom and prosperity that have surpassed the wildest hopes of other regions and times, will rapidly fade away into stagnation, poverty and ruin and almost certainly into a brutal and lawless tyranny.

We have seen in this century the collapse and dissolution of once mighty empires and the falling into decadence and violence of their inhabitants. In every case their social and political destruction was accompanied by financial irresponsibility and extravagance, and the disappearance of sound money. So it will be with us, if we do not take heed now. If we go down in that fashion, historians will record that it was due to the greed and selfish indifference of the people—those who did not care enough to ensure the survival for their children and their grandchildren, of the beautiful society and great nation the founding fathers strived to create.

If we are to accomplish the task of ending uncontrolled inflation, then all of us whether we are in politics, business or a skilled craft, must stop following the path of abject surrender in our daily actions, to personal or political or ideological expediency. We must devote our whole lives to preventing the threatened catastrophe and subordinate many considerations of personal expediency.

Ever since the war in Vietnam expanded, we have had a spate of articles and some do-it-yourself books on "how to live with inflation." The authors suggested investments in common stocks, precious metals and gems, fine paintings and rare coins, and in carefully chosen real estate as hedges against the ravages of inflation. Even rare vintage wines were proposed as hedges. Some authors suggested resorting to barter trading, or escape to remote parts of the globe where the cost of living is very low.

Others dealt with more sophisticated techniques for coping with inflation; how to pick out the best investments in mining and manufacturing industries, and commerce and finance areas, both in the United States and abroad, that stood to profit by inflation. We had a tremendous wave of speculation in gold bars as a result of all this how-to-live-with-inflation agitation. Very few people so far have made money out of gold. Even if they bought before the big price rise and sold before the inevitable declines, they found out that the cost of warehousing and insuring gold ate up their profits.

Some industrialists and speculators made money by hoarding stocks of strategic industrial and commercial commodities. Many of the speculators and legitimate businesses suffered big losses when their necessary hedging operations were disrupted by the feverish speculation induced by uncontrolled inflation.

You can exist under uncontrolled inflation, but you aren't really living because unrestrained inflation pollutes life, corrupts its flavor and weakens or destroys its purpose.

Even thinking in terms of living with severe inflation is an ignoble and cowardly surrender, a betrayal of all the sound virtues and principles on which our American society is based. Instead of prattling glibly about living with inflation, we should realize that the only way to exist with uncontrolled inflation is to fight it every minute of every day with all the intellectual and moral vigor we possibly can muster.

Otherwise, unrestrained inflation can and will reduce life in America to empty, impoverished misery, a society with vastly more corruption, ignorance, crime and violence than we have now.

To conquer uncontrolled inflation will require a better and more objective understanding of inflation than even our best informed economists, financiers and political leaders appear to have today. Our worst failure in dealing with inflation is to take a didactic, even a moralistic view of it. We look at uncontrolled inflation not as a natural and inevitable phenomenon, which history plainly shows it to be, but as a plague visited upon mankind by Satan. So long as we continue to hold this deluded view, our measures to deal with inflation will continue to be inept.

Uncontrolled inflation is indeed a plague. If paper money had been in use in biblical times, Saint John undoubtedly would have listed inflation as a fifth horseman in his apocalyptic vision in the book of Revelation, along with war, famine, pestilence and death as the great scourges of mankind. Inflation did occur in biblical times. An historical novelist suggested not long ago that inflation may have played a significant role in the crucifixion of Jesus. He portrayed Pontius Pilate as having wrecked the economy of Judea by an ambitious and gradiose public works program. This brought about a tremendous price inflation, and consequently, Pilate's expenses were so great he used up all the province's tax revenues, leaving nothing to remit to Caesar. Desperate for money, the only one to whom Pilate could turn for a big enough loan was Caiaphas, the chief high priest. When Caiaphas demanded Jesus's execution as payment, Pilate was forced to yield, although he did not believe Jesus had violated either Roman or Jewish law.

Inflation is as natural and as all-pervading as the wind that alternately blows icy gales, pleasant zephyrs and scorching blasts. It also is as natural as the rain that makes all things grow, but can suddenly create floods that drown thousands and wash away homes, factories and farms.

We cannot control the winds, but we can make use of them and we can take shelter against them. We cannot prevent or bring about rain, but we can take maximum advantage of it. Man has learned a great deal about flood control and harnessing the vast power of streams, lakes and even the seas. We must learn to exercise the same degree of control over inflation.

Americans have never had to endure galloping inflation, the kind that wipes out fortunes overnight and reduces whole populaces to hunger. We did have regional "greenback" inflation in the nineteenth century. Some banks issued currency without adequate backing causing commodity price inflation during World Wars I and II. But these were short-lived and easily brought under control.

The first uncontrolled inflation in our history started during the 1960s. President Lyndon Johnson unwisely expanded and intensified the war in Vietnam without putting the country on a war economy. The war, in consequence, proved a bottomless pit into which we poured money, arms and men in vain. Inflation continued to rage uncontrolled in the first Nixon Administration because of the slow pace Nixon followed in winding the war down.

Our help to Israel in the brief third Arab-Israeli war (a popular cause to most Americans), the Arabs' retaliating oil embargo, and the big boost in the global oil price sent inflation soaring to new highs from which it did not drop until the recession of 1975–76.

The impact of this was felt by all Americans. The cost of food went up substantially but prices of nearly everything else went up much faster. The quality and variety of everyday life suffered as small businesses failed. Manufacturers and large merchandisers were forced to trim their product lines and inventories to the bone. Some kinds of goods and services we had taken for granted for generations became unavailable, or were priced out of reach of all except the most fortunate. This harsh rationalizing process threw several million persons out of work and doubled the normal statistical unemployment rate to 8.5 per cent

In Newark, New Jersey, New York City and other communities having a large concentration of disadvantaged minorities, the unemployment reached between 15 and 20 per cent.

A man to cut the lawn or a kitchen maid, adequate automobile and some kinds of liability insurance, extensive highway travel, one-family homes, larger apartments, and personal services are among the things inflation is increasingly putting out of reach of people on salaries or fixed income. Stores can no longer afford to stock the wide selections of merchandise they used to.

Uncontrolled inflation would be disastrous enough if

we only suffered its direct economic consequences, but that is not the case. It has done more than anything else to spread the flames of corruption, crime and terror in the world today.

Uncontrolled inflation is the most potent social catalyst man ever originated. It causes violent interaction between destructive forces that otherwise would remain isolated and relatively manageable. But inflation is usually the catalyst and not the ultimate cause of corruption, crime or terror. A modest amount of inflation appears to have been the price of social progress throughout man's history. Without some inflation there could have been no gradual redistribution of wealth, no upward social mobility of the working man from the manacled slavery of the ancient world to today's prosperous worker.

Today's sophisticated and diversified economy could not have developed without a gradual but steady increase in the money supply. The invention of paper currency, was quickly followed by a tremendous expansion of credit. Then came the discovery of mechanisms for capitalizing assets on the basis of their earning power instead of their cost and obvious functional value, and for capitalizing the purchasing power of workers.

All of these things would have been regarded as highly inflationary and dangerous by the classical economists of the seventeenth and eighteenth centuries. However, in combination with the achievements of science and technology, they have turned the world around. Where once 90 per cent of the people dwelt in grinding poverty during an average life span of only thirty years, modern man lives a relatively prosperous life wherein persons of many countries live more than seventy years.*

However, these expansive economic mechanisms have happy results only as long as they are kept under control. When the controls break down, the money supply expands in a grotesque fashion and the prices of everything rise fantastically. This condition has caused and will continue to cause the most intense human misery.

Uncontrolled inflation aggravates virtually every other social ailment. It proves a tremendous incentive to business, professional, political and personal corruption; also to the widespread destruction of morals and ethics. For many persons it can make working at a steady job appear futile and stupid. It makes resorting to crime seem like the only way to avoid frustration or even starvation.

Inflation creates other desperate frustrations and encourages some persons to turn to terrorism. Uncontrolled inflation also corrupts family life because it distorts values by never manifesting itself in an even manner to all prices and wages. If a family's income is bloated by inflation, extravagance is sure to result. The children will then grow up with exaggerated ideas of the value of material things. If the inflation bears harshly on a family, the children will feel deprived. On seeing other families prosper by inflation they will

*See *You Are Worth a Fortune* by Arthur Milton, Citadel Press, Secaucus, N.J., 1977.

begin to feel that society is totally unjust, and in their self-pity, will become cynical.

Monetary and price chaos is bound to cause bitter squabbling between husbands and wives. Fights over money, or the lack of it, cause far more divorces than infidelity.

The world had examples of galloping inflation in the eighteenth century, caused by the lack of scientific and economic know-how. Reckless speculation in ventures such as John Law's Mississippi Bubble in France and the South Seas Bubble in England resulted in financial disaster.

Law, a Scotsman, was the best mathematician of his day, but he was economically naive by modern standards. He persuaded Philippe d'Orleans, regent for the boy king Louis XV that everyone in France could become rich by floating shares in a company to exploit the wealth of the vast Mississippi Valley, which France then owned. The frenzied speculation that followed did appear to make most Frenchmen rich, and it caused a sudden runaway wave of price inflation that pushed the cost of living sky high. Neither Law nor his French associates had the faintest idea of the real obstacles they faced in developing the Mississippi Valley, and the "bubble" soon burst.

A very similar inflationary bubble was blown a year or so later by British promoters. Their scheme was to trade, mine, and colonize in the islands of the South Pacific and Indian Ocean. This bubble also collapsed, bankrupting thousands after having temporarily inflated England's economy outrageously.

At the end of the eighteenth century, the English clergyman-economist Thomas Robert Malthus warned the world of the inflationary consequences of trying to raise the standard of living in defiance of the law of supply and demand. Malthus did not speak of inflation, though. He simply taught that raising the living standards of the workers would only result in an over-rapid growth of population. This increase, he stated, in the number of mouths to feed would always outrun the growth of the food supply.

For a long time in the nineteenth century, and the first half of this century, Malthus's views appeared to be discredited. Rapid advances in agricultural and industrial technology, accompanied by advances in transportation and the development of refrigeration and other methods of food preservation, enabled production of everything to outstrip population growth. After World War II, this growth in output slowed down while population growth accelerated greatly. The life span then lengthened as a result of medical advances. It soon became apparent that inflating the number of people in the world is quite as dangerous as inflating money; it can lead equally to high prices and a high incidence of corruption and crimes.

That we live in an era of widespread crime and corruption and much terrorism cannot be denied. Crime is certainly much more prevalent in the United States now, than at any time in this century. Of course, we have had more lawlessness in some past eras; just before and during the Revolutionary and Civil wars for example. There was much more crime and turbulence on the western frontier in the last half of the nineteenth century than we have today. Nevertheless, in recent years the streets of our big cities and even much of suburban and rural America have become unsafe at night. People fear the muggers, rapists, perverts, psychotics and gangs of juvenile and not-so-young delinquents, who live by violence and rip-off burglary.

The spreading use of narcotics; the prevalence of violence and pornography on television, in the movies and popular books and magazines; the decline of religious influence; degeneracy in the educational world and the frightening permissiveness of our society. The high degree of mobility; the easy communications and increased density that give the criminal so much opportunity to melt undetected into the crowd, all have a large impact on the crime rate. Yet the record shows plainly that the growth of crime in America accelerated enormously, precisely during those years when inflation was least under control.

Crime, of course, is more continuous than inflation. We must live with crime even in times of deflation. Nevertheless, the Congressional Joint Economic Committee led by Sen. Hubert Humphrey, D,—Minn., says crime has grown astonishingly during the inflation of the 1960s and the 1970s. The committee put the total cost of crime to the nation, including the cost of maintaining the courts, at $125 billion a year. Surprisingly, it found that the biggest single item in this bill is not the violent crime of the gangsters and juvenile delinquents, but business and white collar crime, for which the committee put the annual bill at $44 billion. This covers bogus bankruptcies, other frauds, stock jobbing, kickbacks, bribery, embezzlement, computer crime and direct price rigging.

That business crime has more direct inflationary impact on the economy than crimes of violence seems axiomatic. What is less clear, is the matter of how much business crime is the result of temptations and pressures created by inflation. Certainly that amount must be substantial.

Computer crime is the newest element in business crime. It is definitely a cause rather than a symptom of inflation. The outstanding example of computer crime was the Equity Funding Corporation scandal a few years back.

One of the worst examples of computer crime, one that still is growing, is the fraudulent federal income tax refund racket. It is thus far known to be siphoning more than $5 million a year out of the national treasury. The con artist takes advantage of the electronic computer's stupidity, its inability to make a value or judgment decision. He gets a large number of income tax return blanks and W-2 withholding tax forms. He then files a big batch of totally fictitious income tax returns, each requesting a refund of several hundred or even several thousand dollars. As long as he does not make one of those obvious procedural or mathematical mistakes the computer is programmed to catch, the electronic monster will order the refunds paid. By the time the swindle is discovered, the con man has collected his money and vanished. To the Internal Revenue Service's great chagrin, it was learned that this racket was worked quite successfully by a group of convicts in the Federal Penitentiary at Leavenworth, Kansas.

A huge increase in the incidence of arson can be blamed almost entirely on uncontrolled inflation. The grossly inflated valuations on buildings, including homes, merchandise and industrial stocks tempts many people to insure the properties to the hilt and then hire firebugs to torch them.

Walter D. Swift, a vice president of the American Insurance Association, said the direct cost of arson to insurance companies hit $1.2 billion in 1976, roughly half the year's fire loss! He added that the number of arson fires is increasing by 20 to 25 per cent a year. Counting employment, business failure losses and the cost of additional fire protection, Swift believed the real cost of arson to the nation in 1976 was more than $20 billion.

Most arson is carried out by professionals but amateurs do a lot of the torching, especially where residential fires are concerned. The risk of prosecution is small, because the authorities simply haven't the manpower to properly investigate the tidal wave of suspicious fires and neither do the insurance companies. Swift calculated that only one per cent of the deliberately set fires in the United States result in arrest and conviction. The owners of torched properties often protect themselves by putting legal title to the properties in straw names and setting themselves up to collect as mortgagees.

So-called victimless crimes also have increased enormously during the inflationary years. Actually there are no victimless crimes; if no one else is victimized, the offender victimizes himself or herself. This is particularly true of prostitution, which always becomes more prevalent in times of severe inflation. Usually young women with inferior backgrounds, low intelligence or inadequate schooling, have difficulty finding steady employment at a living wage. When the eagerness of weak, vicious men to prey on such women by pimping fills the streets with hookers and call girls, money and steady wages lose their value.

Narcotics peddling, numbers running and other illegal gambling activities, also called victimless crimes, increase similarly as inflation spreads. There are persuasive arguments for decriminalizing both prostitution and the use of certain narcotics, and these arguments are heard with growing frequency as inflation multiplies. The swelling army of pimps, dope pushers and corrupt law enforcement officers engaged in the cruel exploitation of the hustlers and junkies increases the blight of inflation.

During the same inflation-ridden years, corruption became more pervasive in every layer of American society. Of course, ethical styles change from generation to generation. Gen. Andrew Jackson thought there was nothing wrong in getting a whole battalion of militia roaring drunk and marching them to the polls to vote for Old Hickory. That would scandalize us.

"Let the buyer beware" and "Charge all the traffic will bear" were slogans preached by even the most respectable nineteenth century businessmen. The elder J. Pierpont Morgan, a deeply religious and enlightened man, insisted that the operation of his huge international banking firm was "none of the public's damned business." Trading in slaves and opium was eminently respectable in the early nineteenth century. Marketing the kind of pornographic and violent entertainment that is acceptable today would have caused a man to be ostracized as late as the early 1940s.

On balance, though, it appears that many more persons are "on the take" now than at any time in our past. Larger sums are involved, and the forms of corruption are often more sinister and socially destructive. The incentive that has lured and driven so many persons into these corrupt practices, is the desperate need or greed for money to cope with uncontrolled inflation's skyrocketing prices.

Since Watergate, virtually no one will deny that corruption of the government in the United States has increased enormously. No one with rudimentary intelligence is deceived into believing that the ouster of President Nixon (on a huge pension and financial allowances), and the meager punishments for the other Watergate offenders, is sufficient enough to have any great deterrent effect on political corruption. This corruption has been shown to be all pervasive, extending from the White House, through the governmental bureaucracy, down through the judiciary and Congress to state and local governments and the military.

Curiously, there is one area of government where corruption has diminished almost to the vanishing point—the ballot. The voting machine and the electronic computer have made it virtually impossible to steal an election. You cannot rig the machines. It is much too difficult to marshal enough illegal voters to affect the election results decisively.

Some observers insist that business corruption has not increased much. They say that only a great deal more is being discovered. Those who feel that way, say the overseas bribery scandals involving Lockheed Aircraft, Gulf Oil, Ashland Oil and scores of other corporations, simply would have been ignored or taken for granted a generation back. But they resulted in the ouster of the chairmen of two of these giant companies. Many other executives and prime ministers of two great countries, were similarly disgraced.

The editors of the eminent *Harvard Business Review*, take a dim view of the complacency over business corruption. They concluded in December, 1976, on the basis of a questionnaire sent to 1,227 representative executives of big firms that there has been a definite increase in corruption and a decline in ethical standards in America since 1961. This was about the time uncontrolled inflation began to gather force. The magazine conducted a similar study of American business ethics that year. In the new study, only 32 per cent of the respondents actually said there had been a decline in ethics. Another 41 per cent said there had been no improvement. The principal complaint of those who thought corruption was spreading, was that they encountered frequent pressure from their superiors to sign false documents; to do business with the boss's friends; to overlook clearly wrongful acts by superiors;

plus pressure to support viewpoints that obviously were incorrect. Other corrupt practices complained of, included bribes and kickbacks; "loans granted as favors"; substitution of materials in orders without the customers' knowledge, and a wide variety of misrepresentations about the quality of products and the terms of sales and delivery schedules. More than half the executives said their superiors did not want to know how results were achieved, so long as the revenue kept rolling in.

What the Harvard editors found most disturbing was, while 42 per cent of the respondents said they themselves would refuse to pay bribes, only nine per cent felt that the average executive was above paying or taking bribes.

Some of the most serious corruption that has grown up in the inflationary era is a direct creation of state legislatures and even of the voters—the legalization of gambling on a huge scale in the form of lotteries, casinos and offtrack betting on horse racing to raise tax revenues. It is certainly true that people will gamble whether or not it is permitted. It also is true that different segments of the population have widely differing ideas about the morality of gambling. The puritanical refusal of the Protestant majority in the past, to countenance any form of legal betting or gaming, left the whole business of gambling largely in the hands of criminals.

Nevertheless, the growing legalization of gambling has increased the amount of corruption in state and local politics. This also is a product of uncontrolled inflation. Before severely inflated costs of government services made them so desperate for revenue, the politicians and bureaucrats would not have dared ask the voters to approve anything so wasteful and demoralizing as public lotteries and offtrack betting on horseraces.

A considerable number of persons believe that the official sanction given to call options trading by the Securities and Exchange Commission, and the actual engaging in options trading by three of the country's larger stock exchanges, is a definite manifestation of corruption in American society. Even the prestigious New York Stock Exchange has announced it expects to permit its facilities to be used for options trading, and the SEC recently has been reported to permit trading in put (sell) options as well as calls (buy options).

Buying and selling stocks and commodity futures on margin also is criticized as gambling. It does provide a speculative cushion for the market, and producers and traders in commodities do have to hedge their operations against sudden price changes. Therein, margin trading serves a useful function. However, it can get out of control and result in reckless gambling as the scandal in the Maine potato futures market demonstrated, back in 1976.

It is not possible to show that trading puts and calls is anything other than pure gambling. Nor can anyone deny that gambling has a corrupting influence on society. The big boom in options has coincided with uncontrolled inflation. People are attracted to trade in the options market in the hope of making easy money to offset the impact of inflation on their other affairs.

Domestic terrorism never has been big in the United States, except when it was practiced against blacks in the South during the Reconstruction Era. We never had anything like the terrorism that in recent years has afflicted Vietnam, Argentina, Northern Ireland, Lebanon and so much of the rest of the world. Lately though, we have had to cope with a rise in international and transnational terrorism. In a rather detailed report made public in April, 1976, the Central Intelligence Agency noted that 40 per cent of the targets of international and transnational terrorist acts around the world, involving kidnappings, bombings, assassinations, skyjackings and the like, were American business firms or American individuals. Our great wealth and our devotion to free enterprise democracy, and our antisocialist economics gives us an overwhelming symbolic value as a target in the eyes of political terrorists.

The CIA noted in the study, that international terror (terrorist activities initiated or condoned by governments), and transnational terror (activities of private terrorists that cross national boundaries), always increase in times when money is plentiful. It is mainly in such inflationary times that the terrorists can raise the money to buy arms and explosives and be able to finance their rather expensive activities.

By now, many readers must believe that I am indicting the very American social system which I am trying to defend against the ravages of inflation. I do indeed seek to indict those aspects of the system as it works presently. I have the deepest reverence for the American way of life and our social system as it was until about twenty years ago. I want to salvage that system for my children and your children and our children's children.

2.

INFLATION AND ARMAMENTS

Some years ago an international wit said, "When the nations wish to disarm, they hasten to do so—when they don't wish to, they hold a disarmament conference."

Nobody has been trying hard to talk up a disarmament conference recently, except the Russians. If the international wit was right, it is the Russians who really do not want to disarm. The armaments race is certainly the most important cause of uncontrolled inflation in the world.

Gen. Alexander Haig, the top commander of North Atlantic Treaty Organization forces, insisted on January 9, 1977, that the Russians are building up their military bases to a degree that threatens the security of the western world. Haig said the Soviet buildup was so great that the deterrent forces NATO has maintained for twenty-seven years might ultimately be destroyed.

General Haig's views would carry far more weight with the American people, if it were not for his long personal association with Richard Nixon and the Pentagon-industrial juggernaut. Secretary of State Henry Kissinger flatly contradicted General Haig and a team of CIA officials who had been voicing a similar opinion.

Kissinger said: "I do not believe the Soviet Union is achieving military superiority over the United States—I do not believe any American administration would permit a situation to arise in which the Soviet Union could achieve military strategic superiority over the United States." He went on to say that "the essence of the situation is that military superiority has no practical significance when casualties on both sides would be in the tens of millions, as long as we do what is necessary to maintain the balance."

Kissinger defined "what is necessary" as "strengthening U.S. forces that would be involved in regional conflicts" which, he said, are the real military danger facing the country.

Since our abortive war in Vietnam and since seeing the republican government in South Korea degenerate into a dictatorship, accused of spending a lot of money to bribe members of the U.S. Congress, Americans are pretty fed up with regional conflicts. It would take some crass and overt move by the Russians, the mainland

Chinese, or the Cubans to get us into any military adventures in Africa, for example.

But the old chestnut that "when Wall Street sneezes, Europe catches pneumonia" is paralleled by what happens when the United States inflates its economy in order to arm half the globe, as we have been doing in recent years. With the exception of the oil exporting countries, there are few nations on earth that have the opportunity to control their own economic destinies. This is particularly true of the developing countries. The rapid rise in prices of manufactured things, consumer products as well as machinery and other installations for industry is fast and steady. The prices of the commodities they produce go up much more slowly.

This leads to widespread misery, to desperation and to extreme political radicalism followed by wholesale commercial, financial and political corruption, hatred of foreigners, expropriation of foreign enterprises and ultimately to violence and terror. It also leads to civil wars and the rise of dictatorships, both rightist and leftist.

The revolts of the peoples of Africa and Asia against their European colonial overlords were inevitable. It was inevitable that some or most of the republics created in the erstwhile colonies would degenerate into some form of feudal dictatorship, or succumb to communist conquest. This process was accelerated tremendously by inflation in the United States and western Europe, starting in the 1960s. The United States' war in Vietnam had a disastrous impact all over the world, because the struggle sent American price levels soaring. Both President Johnson and President Nixon were preoccupied with the Vietnam conflict. This preoccupation kept Washington from listening to the pleas for help and understanding from so many of the peoples of the rest of the world.

Because the communists were thwarting us and humiliating us in Vietnam, we Americans became almost hysterical in our opposition to virtually any social and economic reform that the communists encouraged anywhere in the world. Our fear and distrust of Russia, China and Cuba became a fear of anyone who wanted to change the status quo anywhere. The global inflation was created largely by our military adventures, and the consequences of this inflation were making the need for radical social reform imperative in large areas. We exported misery along with our inflation, an inflation of 11 per cent a year in the United States that swiftly became 25 to more than 100 per cent a year in some of the developing lands.

Simultaneously the United States began enormous export sales of weapons and munitions to countries ruled by "anti-communist" governments. We did this to keep our huge aerospace and armaments industries operating on a large scale in order not to maintain a huge surplus productive capacity in idleness. The Pentagon, the Johnson and Nixon administrations desired this surplus capacity in order to maintain high employment and high profits for industry, and to have a big war materiel capacity ready in case of a showdown with Russia.

One expert has estimated the maintenance cost of excess productive capacity in the aircraft industry alone at $250 million a year. Many persons may believe that keeping this excess aircraft building capacity is a necessary gamble. But we should remember President Eisenhower's warning against the political danger of allowing a huge military-industrial establishment to become permanent. Eisenhower's warning was elaborated by Prof. Seymour Melman of Columbia University in his book, *The Permanent War Economy*.

The export of billions of dollars worth of American planes, tanks, guns and other arms has aggravated inflation even in prosperous Iran. This inflation has aroused some strong resentment against the United States on the part of those Iranians who look on Shah Mohammed Reza Pahlevi with something less than enthusiasm. These republican-minded Iranians do not believe their country any longer is seriously menaced by Russia. They are convinced that the Shah really wants his huge army and air force and his stupendous arsenal of weapons, mainly to keep himself in power and assure the succession of his young son, or to attack Iraq and Saudi Arabia. They think that, by selling arms to the Shah, the United States simply is creating an inflation in Iran that is robbing the Iranian people of the fruits of their oil and their labor.

Historically, dictators of all political shades have been notoriously fickle where allies are concerned. Josef Stalin did not hesitate to betray Britain and France by making an alliance with Hitler (which eventually backfired). Can we trust the Asian and Latin-American dictators we have armed to the teeth, at the cost of great inflationary burdens for their peoples and ourselves, not to join forces someday with our adversaries and turn those weapons against us?

We have not won the friendship of the peoples to whose governments we have sold huge amounts of arms, except for Israel. Nor are the governments our friends. We have supplied both the Greeks and the Turks, who are traditional enemies, with large amounts of arms. Both nations have come close to full scale war in recent years over Cyprus, and both nations insistently clamor for more arms and each accuses us of favoring the other. Even the Israelis often act as if it were self-evident that the survival of the United States depends on the survival of Israel, and that gives them a permanent blank check on the U.S. Treasury.

Our big sales of arms to South Korea, the Philippines, Thailand and various Latin-American governments have earned us intense dislike from the downtrodden populaces of those countries. Those peoples see the weapons used only to perpetuate the rule of strong-man governments. It is the common people that have to suffer to pay for the arms and then suffer the burden of the resulting inflation.

In some of these countries, the armaments burden eats up a quarter or more of the gross national income, yet these nations have not been involved in real foreign wars for generations, and have no genuine external enemies. The very existence of big armed establishments in these countries prevents economic or social progress and makes revolution and terrorism likely to break out.

It is necessary for us to maintain an up-to-date armaments industry in the United States. But that we should supply all the arms for the free enterprise lands is highly debatable. The French, for example, are very eager to sell arms to whoever will buy them, and our pious objections to some recent French sales of arms are a prime example of the pot calling the kettle black. The Soviet Union does not supply all arms for the communist world; China, Czechoslovakia and East Germany contribute substantially. Nor do the Russians finance the armaments of the communist world to the degree that we finance armaments for western countries. The Russians do grant large credits for arms to the Arab nations for use against Israel.

Much of the money to pay for American arms sent abroad has come immediately out of the pockets of American taxpayers. Even if the foreign buyers agree to pay big prices for the weapons, the U.S. government guarantees the loans, and the sales are mostly handled through our armed forces.

As a rule, the foreign nations get U.S. arms at bargain prices, either for political reasons or because the planes and weapons sold are aging surplus munitions. These arms can be quite useful to a government putting down a rebellion of peasants and workers, but of extremely limited value against a modern army in the field. Our Defense Department doubtlessly calculates that it is making a profit by selling these weapons at any price. Otherwise, they simply would have to be junked in time. One real purpose of the sales is to get rid of large stores of older weapons. This helps justify the generals' and admirals' placing of orders for billions of dollars worth of new weapons, many of which may turn out in the long run to be costly and useless. Those who favor junking the controversial B-1 bomber say it is likely to be merely a $100 billion toy for the men with stars on their shoulders, and will have no real military value. In that case, its impetus to further inflation is obvious.

Many persons are convinced that the U.S. sale of arms abroad cannot be reduced, at least not rapidly, without bringing on a serious depression here at home. This too is quite debatable. There are many things American taxpayers could spend their money on that would create more jobs, earn better profits for industry, and do more for the quality of life than selling arms. Selling arms is just an easy way for industry to show a profit with minimum risk.

In January 1975, the Federal Bureau of Labor Statistics said in a report ignored by President Ford that while $1 billion spent to produce arms created fifty-one thousand jobs, the same amount spent on housing created sixty-one thousand jobs, and $1 billion spent on manpower training would put one hundred and thirty-six thousand people to work. Other government studies showed, that of the ninety-six million Americans actively employed in 1975, a total of seven million owed their jobs to the Pentagon and/or defense related industries. These were by all odds the most costly jobs in the country to maintain. Moreover, in true economic sense, they are totally unproductive, hence they serve mainly to inflate the economy. These jobs include 2.1 million men and women in uniform; one million civilian employees of the armed forces; 1.7 million employed in military research and development; 2.2 million in jobs dependent on the trickle-down effect of defense spending.

The fact that these people are not productive in the true economic sense, does not mean that many of them are not essential to national welfare. The problem is to determine what constitutes adequate defense and how many of these seven million jobs are really needed.

Cost overruns are one of the worst inflationary aspects of defense. Prof. Robert Fox of the Harvard Business School, formerly an assistant secretary of the Army, says cost overruns amount to several billion dollars a year. The Washington Center for Defense Studies, a private research group, recently calculated that the makers of forty-six weapons currently under contract, piled up a $61 billion bill for inadequately explained cost overruns.

Defense spending also has discriminatory consequences on the economy. It tends to provide jobs for skilled factory workers (who were the biggest bloc—24 per cent—of the unemployed), but offered little help to untrained workers in 1975. Dr. Roger Bezdek of the University of Illinois, has charged that defense spending also gives a disproportionate share of federal contract work to the southern states, while the eastern and midwestern states, where jobless rates are much higher, get very few of the defense dollars.

In spite of the necessity of maintaining armed forces and a defense industry, it is obvious that arms spending is the one completely controllable inflationary element in our economy. Every penny spent on arms must be approved by Congress every year. No manufacturer may sell arms abroad without an export license, and Congress determines what arms may be sold and how the sales may be financed.

The inflationary impact of big armaments on the economies of the rest of the world, is greater than the burden on the United States, even though Americans and Russians produce most of the arms. In a letter to *The New York Times,* Norman E. Hunt, executive director of World Federalists Association, said sixty million persons around the world were either in uniform or working in munitions plants in 1976. Total military expenditures on earth in 1976 were well above $300 billion. Hunt recalled that in the 1960 presidential election, a big issue was the "missile gap" between the United States and the Soviet Union. After he entered the White House, President Kennedy said he learned the missile gap never had existed. Hunt claimed the Pentagon-industrial combine "anticipated (President) Carter's economies and peace initiatives," and built up a bogeyman like they had in the 1950s missile gap. Hunt said the generals, admirals and defense officials wanted to head off defense economies and peace initiatives. Hunt also stated that President Carter's efforts to reduce armaments "may be the last chance for a peaceful world." They may also be the last chance to stop uncontrolled inflation.

In the closing days of his term, President Ford submitted to Congress a budget for fiscal 1978. He called for expenditures of $440 billion and a deficit of $47 billion. The request for defense outlays was $111 billion, up 12 per cent from the outlays for fiscal 1977. Although officials of the incoming Carter Administration said the proposed defense outlays could be cut, they didn't say by how much.

The obvious lesson to be drawn from any cool-headed thinking about inflation and armaments is, except for such bizarre follies as John Law's Mississippi Bubble, uncontrolled inflation today is what it has been throughout history—a reflex of war or of the fear of war.

It has occurred on a prolonged basis only at times when rulers were spending an inordinate portion of their gross national income on armies, navies and armaments. There has been severe inflation, of course, at times when there was no immediate peril of war: the German galloping inflation in the early 1920s, French and Italian inflation in the mid-1920s, all were reflexes of World War I's political and economic disruptions. The really significant fact is, they did not continue for long but were brought under control rather easily.

The whole free enterprise system has lived since World War II under the threat of another vaster war. This period has been marked by numerous costly, savage smaller wars: the Greek civil war; three Arab-Israeli wars; the Korean war; wars in Indo-China; the revolt of Bangladesh against Pakistan; civil wars in Cyprus and Lebanon; guerrilla warfare in Argentina and Northern Ireland, and numerous savage conflicts in Africa in which many thousands perished.

From none of these conflicts has the United States been able to remain aloof and uninvolved. Therein lies the root cause of our recent periods of uncontrolled inflation. Who can doubt that if there had been no third Arab-Israeli war, there would have been no 1973 oil embargo and no sudden increase in the global oil prices to spur inflation everywhere?

Fear of war does not necessarily mean fear of attack by a foreign enemy. Argentina, Brazil, Chile and Mexico have no reason to fear involvement in external armed struggles. Yet all have had fearful inflation in recent years, while West Germany and Finland, which must live next door to the Soviet Union, and have fought the Russians within recent memory, have had relatively little inflation. This is not really a paradox. The four Latin American countries all are wracked by extreme social tensions and guerrilla warfare and by the constant threat of civil war. West Germany and Finland have very stable societies except for a small terrorist movement in Germany.

Other countries whose frontiers seem quite safe, and who are not threatened with civil war, are also experiencing severe inflation. But in every case it is easy to demonstrate that their economies and trading patterns are gravely perilled by war or the threat of war anywhere in the world.

3.

LIVING OVER A VOLCANO

Nowhere has excessive inflation destroyed the quality of life so much as in our bigger U.S. cities.

It has made life horribly unsafe for millions of persons, because it has increased crime and violence. It has also raised costs so much, that it has forced a shocking neglect of maintenance of buildings; public transit equipment; and street repair in urban environs. This has resulted in a big increase in fires and tragic accidents.

The passage of the stiff Federal Occupational Safety and Health Act prevented a similar rise in accidents in industrial and commercial premises. Ironically, OSHA also has had an inflationary impact. It has raised costs for all industrial and many commercial businesses, and forced some small companies to simply throw in the towel.

It is safe to assert that thousands of lives have been lost in fires and other disasters. These disasters simply would not have occurred, had maintenance standards for buildings, railways and other mass transit, gas and power lines, not suffered because of unrestrained inflation. Aged and obsolete equipment is no longer replaced promptly, because excessive inflation has run replacement costs up far above the reserves set in past years to pay for new equipment.

Apartment buildings in the worst slums of our major cities were better maintained back in the 1950s than luxury apartments are today. Statistics of the property and casualty insurance companies show a rise in fire losses somewhat above the mere appreciation of the values of the destroyed properties. The number of persons who lose their lives in fires seems to be rising at an appalling rate.

In the winter of 1976–77 we also had an unusual number of marine disasters that knowledgeable shipping people said appeared to be caused by penny-pinching neglect due to inflation. These accidents were mainly to foreign flag craft, but foreign flag craft entering American harbors often are wholly or partly American owned.

The deterioration of the inner city areas of our metropolitan centers began some years before uncontrolled inflation became acute. Urban decay was already far advanced when the civil rights ferment of the early and middle 1960s, produced the campus and ghetto riots in Los Angeles, Detroit, Washington, Newark, New York and other cities.

Hardly a city in the land had been spared the disastrous consequences of urban sprawl and downtown decay. Some cities were growing so fast that by the simple expedient of extending their limits and annexing new areas, they could offset downtown decay. But for many, this was not the case. The flight of the middle class to the countryside, simply caused tax revenues to dwindle disastrously. By default, the balance of voting power and the burden of governing was thrust on the blacks, Hispanics and other minority elements of the population who often have the least political and administrative experience.

Except in New York, the officials and the citizens of many stricken cities set to work with determination and good will to bring about reform and rehabilitation. They all ran afoul of the uncontrolled inflation of the late 1960s and the 1970s, which soon made most of their problems utterly unmanageable. It became impossible to finance reform and rehabilitation and nearly impossible to keep physical decay and social deterioration from spreading like wildfire. That things have not become much worse, is a great tribute to the devotion and industry of the black mayors and other officials from underprivileged classes elected in the past decade, who have done extremely well against overwhelming odds.

Uncontrolled inflation has taken a cruel toll. A wave of strikes by teachers, transit workers, sanitation men and other municipal employees, even police and firemen, was the first heavy blow. Municipal workers had always been well paid in America. But the rising prices of the 1960s squeezed them hard. Strikes of public workers have long been considered plainly illegal and politically unthinkable, and when attempted in the past had been firmly suppressed. It was the suppression of a police strike in Boston that catapulted Gov. Calvin Coolidge into the vice-presidency, and eventually into the White House.

Many public officials were frightened out of their wits when municipal workers walked off their jobs in the 1960s. Even though the courts issued back-to-work orders, the mayors and other officials still vacillated and failed to enforce the law. A strike at the very start of the administration of Mayor John Lindsay of New York halted the city's vast network of subway and bus lines, forcing millions to walk miles to work. The strike led to a big jump in the transit fare and set an example across the country that was quite disastrous.

The New York subway strike caused a general deterioration of the authority of municipal and state governments. This was followed by a lack of public confidence in elected officials everywhere. It also emboldened leaders of municipal workers unions to make outrageous demands and call unlawful work stoppages. Furthermore, workers were demoralized in municipal departments in many cities and began to feel that they could neglect their duties with impunity. This accelerated cost inflation, and forced tax rates to go up excessively. The municipal workers were to pay a fearful price for these excesses. Cities all across the land were soon caught in such severe financial squeezes that they had to lay off employees. These layoffs ranged from high salaried bureaucrats and school officials, through the ranks of police and firemen, to ordinary clerks and manual laborers.

The New York subway strike had another extremely evil effect. It was followed by bus and trolley strikes, big fare boosts in other cities and even in small towns. This made the cost of riding public transit to and from work prohibitive, or nearly so, for many persons engaged in the lowest paid jobs. Many of these poor people had to travel long distances to work because industry had fled from the inner cities to the suburbs. They also felt forced to move to remote neighborhoods in order to find safety and reasonable rents. Often they had to pay two bus fares to get to work and two to get home. The journey to and from work took so much time out of the day, that some poor families concluded it was no longer worthwhile to work. They then concluded they could live just as well on relief as on the take-home pay from a mean job.

In many smaller communities inflated operating costs simply priced buslines out of existence. That meant that life became almost unbearable in communities without one's own automobile. Without a car, one could not get to and from work; could not get to a hospital or a doctor's office; nor go to church; shop or visit friends without great difficulty. The decline of public transportation naturally caused a vast increase in automobile traffic density in cities and towns. The streets were clogged all day with automobiles carrying only one or two persons. This made parking a frightful problem.

Thousands of small shops and not so small stores and service businesses went broke. Many customers could no longer reach them by bus or find parking spaces for their cars. This forced the surviving businesses to buy additional real estate for parking lots for customers, thus helping to inflate the real estate market. They also had to buy liability insurance for protection against accidents in the parking lots, which soon became the scene of many crimes as well as accidents. The cost of doing business thus was substantially increased, adding to overall economic inflation.

The South and Southwest and some parts of the Far West, have been least afflicted by the changes. Many cities and towns in those regions have prospered and progressed while the eastern and midwestern states have experienced severe setbacks since the 1950s. New York City probably has endured the most calamitous blows of uncontrolled inflation. During the years following the progressive, yet thrifty, administration of Fiorello H. LaGuardia, the city had a succession of spendthrift governments. It seemed their whole philosophy was to pile up debt for the coming generation to pay. The city's bookkeeping was habitually rigged to conceal the true scope and seriousness of the financial situation. Ironically, in their eagerness to cover up waste and deficiencies, the City Hall bureaucrats sometimes succeeded in burying and losing sight of asset accounts amounting to many millions of dollars.

When the day of reckoning finally came under Mayor Abraham Beame, the situation looked even more terrifying than it really was.

The City Hall habit of sweeping unpleasantness under the rug was largely responsible for the subway strike that started the city on its financial toboggan slide. Outgoing Mayor Robert Wagner and incoming Mayor John Lindsay each tried to force the other to take on the harsh responsibility of reaching a settlement with Mike Quill's Transit Workers Union and averting the strike. The union's contract was to expire with the end of Wagner's term and Lindsay kept insisting it was Wagner's duty to settle with the TWU before leaving office. So he refused to take a hand in the talks although Quill warned him that his refusal probably would lead to a strike that could wreck his whole administration. Wagner simply procrastinated, leaving Lindsay to pick up the whole mess. Lindsay, who had represented a silk stocking district in Congress, but had little or no experience in administration, was completely mousetrapped.

The TWU struck and defied a court order to return to work. Mike Quill was jailed. Shortly after, he died of a heart attack.

Although he was reelected for a second term, Lindsay's administration really went down the drain from his first day in office. Much of the city's economic and social health went with it. Lindsay's eight years were marked by strike after strike of teachers, sanitation men and other city workers. The piling of mountains of debt, staggering inflation of the city's army of employees and a huge flight of industry and commerce from New York nearly crushed the city permanently. Towards the end of his term, Lindsay, who had been elected as a Republican, was naive enough to enter the Florida presidential primary as a Democrat.

The facts and figures on the extent of the deterioration of public services in New York make somber reading. A greatly diminished police force is making one-third fewer arrests than two years ago, although crime in the city has not decreased significantly. The streets are not safe at night, nor are many areas in the daytime. The streets are filthy and the sidewalks are jammed with uncollected garbage bags and cans. The sanitation department not only has had the most layoffs of any city service but because the workers are not well enough supervised and are not productive. Too many of them just don't care, and goof off on the job. One-third of the huge fleet of refuse trucks is out of service for lack of maintenance mechanics.

Street repair has suffered horribly. Manhattan Borough President Percy Sutton says he worries about the many bridges in the city that bear the world's heaviest traffic loads. Bridges need constant and complete maintenance or they become dangerous.

The city has cut its budget by $300 million a year, but the state government and the banks, whose help must be forthcoming, along with aid from the Carter Administration, demanded another half billion dollars in economies by the end of 1977, to help prevent the city's bankruptcy.

Subway service has been cut, but not enough to interfere seriously with people's getting to and from work. Yet delays because of disabled trains have become frequent. The number of municipal workers was slashed 19 per cent or 56,000 in 1975 and 1976. Further cuts of 10,000 jobs were projected for 1977. The two biggest services, the schools and the police, were cut the most. The schools lost 12,700 teachers, and the police force about 5,300 officers.

Admittedly, there was considerable fat in all city departments prior to 1975. In some respects the harsh cuts in personnel do not appear to have hampered services greatly. The average time required to answer a police or fire call has not increased noticeably. A 25 per cent cut in city health personnel has been cushioned somewhat by the fact that the city is overbuilt in hospitals and has a surplus of hospital beds.

The deterioration of the public schools, once among the nation's best, however, is conceded to be much more severe than the budget cuts can explain. The number of children of school age in the city has been dropping for some years and, in spite of the economies, the Board of Education still had around 67,000 employees at the end of 1976. Yet many of the schools appeared to be struggling almost hopelessly with disciplinary, racial and other social problems as well as severe curricular difficulties. The competence and motivation of teachers and administrative officers was being widely questioned. It appeared that lack of money was not the most critical evil. Nevertheless, uncontrolled inflation plainly had hurt the schools badly.

Too many young teachers had been laid off; the average age of the teaching force had risen in three years, from twenty-eight to forty-one. Class sizes had mushroomed from twenty to thirty-five. Many schools had no security guards, no hallway or lunchroom monitors and no guidance or vocational counsellors. Most of the nine hundred and eighty-one schools in the system had lost their athletic and recreational programs altogether. There were hardly any bands or other extracurricular activities left. Music, art and remedial courses were whittled away along with sports and physical education.

Another municipal service that has been a casualty of uncontrolled inflation in New York and some other cities is the public parks. The New York Parks Department lost 26.2 per cent of the 4,700 permanent employees in 1975 and 1976, and the parks show it. They began to deteriorate before the inflation, but now both the parks and park employees are unkempt and bedraggled. The parks also are unsafe, infested by hoodlums and perverts.

Inflation has also been the biggest cause of the loss of half a million manufacturing jobs by New York City since 1970. The removal of their headquarters from Manhattan, by many large corporations hasn't helped. Even more disastrous has been the destruction of so many small businesses by inflation.

The severe cutbacks in the schools and the conjunction of inflation and recession have had tragic consequences for thousands of young people who went to college in the late 1960s to prepare themselves to teach. The federal Labor Department yearly issued highly misleading forecasts of the number of teachers that would be needed in the years up to 1980. There did appear to be a shortage of teachers because of the rapid development of the community college movement. "College for everyone," including high school dropouts and middle aged folk who wanted to enrich their lives with more culture, was the order of the day.

But by the end of the 1960s, a gigantic retrenchment was starting. Soon thousands of young people who had master's degrees and teaching certificates were selling house-to-house, driving taxicabs or doing other very ordinary jobs if they were working at all. Their dreams of a life of service in the classroom or the laboratory were in ruins.

As many Americans have been upset by inflation's destructive impact on the postal service as anything else. Other factors played a part, the rapid decline of railway passenger train service, to which the mails had been wedded for generations, and the skyrocketing need for postal services. The department had never been expected to show a profit. But now it ran increasingly into the same law of diminishing returns caused by population density that had made telephone and other public utility services more costly the more customers they acquired. Meanwhile the postal workers were unionized because Congress showed an unwillingness to improve their pay fast enough to keep up with the nation's standard of living.

The early symptoms of postal decay were delayed mails, a drop in postal workers' morale marked by rudeness and shabby, dirty uniforms. The department's once well-kept vehicles became shoddy and ramshackle. The more stamps cost the worse the service seemed to get.

The Nixon Administration conceived the idea of converting the department into a government-sponsored corporation, holding out the hope that by turning the mails over to private business management, things would straighten out and the deficit would vanish. The result was sheer disaster. The first class letter rate climbed to thirteen cents, and postal officials talked of eighteen cents. Parcel post rates went sky high and delivery time stretched from days to weeks. Routine daily home deliveries of mail were cut from two to one and the postal service notified hundreds of small communities their postoffices were to be closed. But local officials and congressmen screamed so loudly that most of the closings were rescinded. At the start of 1977 the postal service, still faced with an enormous deficit, projected at $950 million for fiscal 1978. They then began talking about cutting home deliveries from one a day to three a week, on the dubious plea that the rapid development of electronic communications was eliminating about 40 per cent of the need for first class mail. Mass electronic communications via leased wires by facsimile, videoscreen or teletype have increased greatly and so has use of the long distance telephone. Our once fast and cheap ordinary telegraph system with its army of delivery boys for individual messages is now unbearably slow and expensive, and the messengers have disappeared.

The worst effect uncontrolled inflation has had on city life and on life in many smaller communities, is the frustration created by the widespread and oft concealed ripple effect it has on young people and minority groups. By destroying job opportunities and crippling the schools and social services, it forces many of these people into crime or prostitution, or trying to make a living by gambling or parasitic sycophancy—sponging off well-to-do acquaintances.

This frustration also affects those who are working. It thus creates a seething cauldron of discontent and actual despair and hatred. It makes living in our bigger cities seem like living on top of a live volcano.

4.

THE HEALTH COST SCANDAL

In May 1976, the Federal Council on Wage and Price Stability predicted that the cost of health care would continue to rise faster than the general consumer price index.

In the two years after price controls came off medical care services, up to May, 1976, this cost rose 25.3 per cent in comparison with a 16.4 per cent rise in the CPI. The first big rise in the cost of medical care came some years ago and preceded the spread of corruption and frauds in the medical world. The publicity the corruption has received in recent years is almost enough to make younger persons imagine that the corruption itself caused the cost inflation.

But the corruption has really been a reflex of the infusion of hundreds of millions of dollars of government money into Medicare, Medicaid and the operation of nursing homes. It was marked by many kinds of chiseling, inflated fees and counterfeited billings and by some gross mismanagement and outright stock swindling in the nursing home business.

Although the big cities have seen the most glaring examples of fraud and corruption in health care, abuses have occurred in virtually every part of the country. Many doctors have been caught collecting charges for fictitious patients and fees for services not performed for real patients. Pharmacists, private ambulance firms and other businesses ancillary to the medical world have been involved. Easy money was the lure but inflation increased the toll of the swindles and helped to push the overall cost of medical care ever higher.

The frauds sometime take very ingenious and sophisticated courses. For example, the federal General Accounting Office accused five non-profit firms engaged in providing prepaid Medicaid care in California, of being mere fronts for profit making firms. The GAO said the for-profit companies that controlled the non-profit enterprises, siphoned off large amounts of Medicaid tax funds by various means. The non-profit organizations in question were described as typical prepaid-cost Health Maintenance organizations formed to serve Medicaid patients only.

One particularly dangerous area in health care that can result from inflation is carelessness and fraud in drug testing research. The Food and Drug Administration has been investigating charges that one of the major pharmaceutical houses was guilty of taking serious shortcuts in the laboratory testing of drugs it hoped to get approved for marketing. Rising costs of testing, because of uncontrolled inflation, could tempt the laboratory supervisors to take penny-pinching shortcuts and make false reports on the tests to the government and to the medical profession and the public. The company involved denied vigorously that it had been guilty of shortcuts, but the FDA demanded a full scale grand jury inquiry. The question arises, if one big major company was so careless, how many others were careless but didn't get caught?

Just as serious and more contributory to inflation is the practice in the pharmaceutical industry of bringing out every year, whole series of drugs that are ineffectual and useless. The Food and Drug Administration rarely cracks down on the actual sale of useless drugs, but devotes most of its attention to trying to prevent the sale of dangerous drugs. Of late, both the FDA and Federal Trade Administration have been more active in stopping the pharmaceutical houses from making false claims for useless drugs.

Gouging on fees for minor services is another manifestation of uncontrolled inflation in health care.

Uncontrolled inflation has played a vital, if not dominant, role in what the doctors and hospital administrators call "the rising cost of delivery of medical services." Of course, costs have also gone up for other reasons. Medical science has continued to make great progress in the years since World War II. Many of the most effective procedures and new drugs are inherently very expensive. The cost of educating and training doctors and nurses also has gone up because of inflation and because of the increasing sophistication of the two professions and the greater degree of specialization required. Equipment costs for doctors' offices, hospitals and nursing homes have soared astonishingly.

In consequence, the fees of medical specialists have gone up at least as much as the inflation of money. Fees of general practitioners are about the same as the inflation of money and surgical fees are perhaps a little less. But the cost of a day's stay in a hospital has gone up a lot more than the inflation of the dollar. The question of whether the overall quality of health care has improved or deteriorated during the periods of uncontrolled inflation is very complex. Medical knowledge has improved and health statistics reveal steady declines in the rates of most infectious diseases. A great many more persons are able to get regular medical care today than in the past, but not all the added care is first class.

There is one great irony in the picture. It is the doctors who are most commonly accused of yielding to the temptation offered by the golden flood of government money. But it really is the hospitals, whose administrators seldom are suspected of corruption, that run the cost of health care up the most. This may just mean that the hospitals are victimized by inflation more than the doctors. Hospitals have been forced to reduce their staffs drastically and to shorten duty hours. The nursing profession contends that staff reduction has proceeded to the point where it is dangerous.

Early in 1977, *Nurses 77,* one of the large nursing trade journals, asked ten thousand nurses if they would care to be patients in the hospitals where they worked. An astonishing thirty-eight hundred answered "No." They said staffs had been reduced so much that the chances of serious neglect or dangerous mistakes were grave. Eighteen hundred of the nurses said they knew of cases in which patients had died, because of nurses' errors. An even more astounding 42 per cent of the ten thousand said they knew of patients who had died because of physicians' errors. Four hundred nurses confessed that they themselves had committed errors that contributed to patients' deaths.

Because the case loads are so heavy, nurses often have to wait hours before they can get hold of the needed doctor, and get him to order the procedure they feel is immediately necessary.

"Too much paperwork for nurses" was the next most common complaint. The nurses said this reduced their daily contact with patients far too much.

An extremely critical appraisal of the state of hospital care in our inflationary era is contained in a book entitled *The Unkindest Cut* by Dr. Marie Millman. A professor of sociology in the University of California at Santa Cruz, Doctor Millman spent two years working in hospitals to research the book. She charges that the methods hospitals use or are supposed to use, to prevent and detect culpable medical errors are actually aimed largely at covering them up. This cover up protects negligent and incompetent physicians and nurses against dismissal or malpractice suits. She accused the doctors of "constructing their own ideas of reality" then using these fictions "to ignore and justify medical errors."

Dr. Millman says the chief exculpatory mechanism employed by the doctors is the hospital's monthly medical and morbidity conference, which examines questionable cases. "As one member of the staff after another testifies how he or she was led to the same mistaken diagnosis, the responsibility for the mistake is implicitly spread around. . . . Responsibility is also neutralized by making much of unusual or misleading features of the case or by showing that the patient was to blame because of uncooperative or neurotic behavior," reports Dr. Millman.

I am not directly concerned with the accuracy or inaccuracy of such charges. I am simply pointing out there is a shocking amount of criticism of the current state of health care in hospitals. Much or most of the conditions complained about can be blamed on uncontrolled inflation.

It hardly seems necessary to go into details about how much the cost of health care has risen. Practically everyone has Blue Cross/Blue Shield or a similar kind of health insurance or Medicare, and everyone knows how much the premiums have gone up. The bill for a fairly routine surgical operation requiring a month's stay in the hospital, has jumped in a few years from a little over a thousand dollars to upwards of four thousand. The inflationary impact is the same whether this sum is paid out of the bank account of a well-to-do patient or by Blue Cross/Blue Shield or Medicare or by the city for a charity patient. The soaring prices have precisely the same impact on the economy in each case.

Blue Cross and the other health insurance companies have been waging some valiant efforts to curb the rise in hospital costs. Many hospital administrators and doctors are not giving them the cooperation they need. Public health officials and insurance companies both accuse hospital administrators of not trying to cut overall costs and of encouraging unnecessary admissions and other abuses in order to increase their revenues.

Both New York State and City public officials have been particularly critical of hospital administrators and physicians in this respect.

Dr. Lowell F. Bellin, the city's hospital commissioner, was quoted in *The New York Times*, November 28, 1976: "It's a chaotic and absurd system that can turn honest hospital administrators and physicians into crooks."

A state public health official said the system "had the appearance of fraud". One unnamed doctor was quoted: "A patient comes into my office with a simple stomach pain, so I tell him I have to do a series of tests. He asks me how much the tests will cost. I tell him anywhere from three to four hundred dollars. He then tells me he cannot afford to pay the cost but he does say he is covered by Blue Cross, which would pay him only if he took the tests in a hospital. So he goes in for the tests which easily could be done for less money in my office. I could give you a thousand cases just like it."

The doctor didn't say so, but this hypothetical case appears to involve possible fraud. Many Blue Cross contracts state clearly that Blue Cross is not obligated to pay for diagnostic tests even if they are performed in hospital. So the doctor must attest to an acute condition and state that he knew or suspected this condition in advance of the tests in order for Blue Cross to be obligated. Blue Cross rarely, if ever, questions the doctors' word on this.

City and state officials cited these other cost inflating abuses:

—Patients admitted to hospitals for simple treatment of a rash or removal of a wart.

—Patients admitted only to fill empty beds, and kept longer than really necessary.

—Patients admitted solely for the hospital to realize funds from Medicare, Medicaid or Blue Cross.

The last abuse is important. A municipal hospital administrator explained why. He said Medicaid or Medicare paid his hospital two hundred dollars a day per patient and at that rate he needed to keep 80 per cent of his beds filled to break even. Anything below that put him in trouble and any time he had more than 80 per cent of the beds occupied, the hospital was making money. There is a constant temptation to give a bed to any Medicaid, Medicare or Blue Cross patient who wanted one much of the time. Considering New York state has an acknowledged surplus of five thousand hospital beds, there is real competition for patients. This is a New York state problem, but it exists in varying degrees in many other parts of the country.

There is also a deliberate and cost inflating effort to keep the patients as long as possible. The reason is the hospital makes little or nothing on a patient, even at two hundred dollars a day, right after admission or after surgery, because so much care is required. But the days of the patient's recuperation are "gravy days" when the hospital is making a good profit. One result of this is that the average hospital stay in 1976 was 11.2 days in New York against 7.8 days for the rest of the country. These 3.4 extra days amounted to six hundred and eighty dollars per patient. Federal officials say that cutting one day off the average stay in hospital would save $200 million a year in New York City, and $1 billion across the country. Apparently New York hospitals are doing more to aggravate inflation than all the rest of the hospitals in the country, since those 3.4 extra days waste $680 million per year.

Doctor Bellin said a main cause of the abuses is too much "cost plus" remuneration of the hospitals. "Give them a flat fee for a specific procedure and watch those beds empty out," Dr. Bellin told *The New York Times.*

"Medicaid Mills" or shared health facilities, are also being accused of inflationary fraud in health care. Sen. Frank E. Moss, (D-Utah) in the summer of 1976 charged that Medicaid mills across the country were stealing $1 million a day on fraudulent billings. This means billing the government for office visits and visits to patients' homes that never actually occurred and for various services never performed. This may take the form of inflating the billing for services to real patients or billing for services to patients that never existed. Moss's figure runs to $365 million a year.

Officials in a number of states have obtained indictments against operators of medicaid mills on charges of inflating their billings. Nevertheless, public health officials and consumer organizations generally refuse to get excited about Medicaid mills, saying many of them give as good services to the local communities as older established clinics, and at much lower prices. It is claimed that Medicaid mills are a necessity in poor neighborhoods.

One of the most damaging aspects of health care inflation is its direct impact on business. Every union contract requires the employer to pay a large and varying proportion of each worker's Blue Cross/Blue Shield or similar health insurance premiums. Non-unionized companies have to do the same in order to compete for good workers. In addition to what they pay out for medical insurance, most big companies operate their own clinics providing for emergency services and periodic checkups for their workers. But the big cost burden has always been the insurance premiums.

For some companies skyrocketing health insurance premiums have been great enough to cut substantially into profit. The most dramatic example is Continental Airlines, headquartered in Los Angeles. The company's health insurance bill jumped from $2.12 million for 8,329 employees in 1970, to $7 million for 9,256 employees in 1975. This 197 per cent increase was a great shock to the airline's management, which expected the cost to go up no more than 50 per cent. The hike came at a time when skyrocketing prices of jet fuel were putting red ink all over the books.

A number of other big companies reported staggering, unexpected surges in their health insurance costs for the same five-year period: 100 per cent for Chesebrough-Pond's, the Greenwich, Conn., cosmetic and pharmaceutical house; 94 per cent for Richardson-Merrell, maker of Vick's salves; 91 per cent for Norton Co., the Worcester, Mass., maker of abrasives; 79 per cent for Wm. Wrigley, Jr., Co., the chewing gum manufacturer; 71 per cent for giant PPG Industries, Inc. of Pittsburgh and 55 per cent for Commonwealth Edison, the big Chicago electric utility.

The automobile industry had a 50 per cent rise in health insurance costs negotiated through the United Auto Workers—to an average payment of $150 a month per worker. It's the most comprehensive and liberal medical and hospitalization contract in existence, and the companies pay most of the premiums.

Some big company managements have been so upset by rising health insurance premiums that they switched to self-insurance. Commonwealth Edison was one. The companies that have experienced the really big jumps in health insurance costs almost all blame excessive hospital stays by their workers for lost revenues.

Champion International of Stamford, Conn., a big plywood and paper producer, tried to cut health insurance costs by reimbursing employees for up to $100 of outpatient care. The company believes this will help. A number of Pittsburgh corporations formed a local health planning organization to monitor health and hospital costs in the steel city in an effort to bring prices down.

Somewhat to their surprise, companies that have been trying to do something about skyrocketing health insurance costs drew warm support from President Alexander MacMahon of the American Hospital Association. MacMahon said his association had been trying to put pressure on its own members, the medical profession, the insurance companies and government agencies in order to curb the rising cost of health care and welcomed any help it could get from business firms that had to pay so much of the bill.

5.

BOONDOGGLES AND PIPE DREAMS

If you searched the files of the *Congressional Record,* it wouldn't be hard to come up with enough boondoggles and pipe dreams to suggest that Congress alone has caused the current inflation. That wouldn't be true, but nevertheless its wastes and extravagances have contributed vastly to inflation.

In a democracy such as ours, reckless extravagance cannot occur without the consent and participation of millions of ordinary citizens. Driven by greed or desperate need many people fall into such antisocial activities as chiseling tax monies or engaging in useless activities that waste public funds. All governments in all eras have wrung large sums in taxes from the populace that created vast fortunes for the powerful and privileged. But often as not, the predatory few who benefited by these reckless diversions of public money were themselves thrifty, and put their tainted gains to very practical employment, and this diminished the inflationary effect of the siphoning off of tax funds.

Frequently in the past political graft was more extortionary than inflationary. Instead of spending huge sums on inflationary or visionary projects, the predatory insiders were content to bleed the public treasury by charging high prices for goods and services. They then hoarded their gains so closely that their grafting actually had a deflationary effect on the economy by taking so much money out of circulation. In past centuries, the ruling classes did this deliberately because they had a terrible fear of the lower classes, feeling an urgent need to hold them in subjection keeping society firmly stratified.

Adam Smith, the 18th century economist, put it bluntly when he said the purpose of government was to protect the rich from the poor. The best way to accomplish this was to maintain a very rigid economy with an extremely stable price structure. At all costs, the opportunity for flexible or windfall profits had to be confined to the nobility and the rich. Inflationary trends had to be ruthlessly prevented at any cost including bloodshed, because these trends might let the petite bourgeoisie and the working classes amass wealth and begin to have revolutionary ideas.

This is one of the great differences between society in the modern industrial countries and the peoples who are still living under vestigial feudalism in much of Asia and Latin America. When extravagance becomes rife in a democracy, a great many people manage to get in on a piece of the action.

Most boondoggles are government operations, and the most costly ones require large-scale public participation. The most evident examples are welfare fraud and chiseling on government contracts. The cost of welfare fraud has been reduced somewhat as tight money has forced politicians and bureaucrats to take action . . . but it's still a big drain.

Chiseling on government contracts—federal, state and local—is such a standard practice it hardly seems that anything new can be said about it. It simply adds 10% to 20% to the cost of every particle of goods or services the taxpayers are charged for.

Not all boondoggles are paid for out of tax funds, although nearly all depend on some law or regulation for their operation. One of the longest-lived, biggest boondoggles in American history is almost never heard of outside New York City. It involves investments of about $400 million and it swindles taxicab patrons in the city out of possibly $10 million a year. That's a significant if modest contribution to uncontrolled inflation. It concerns the taxicab medallion licenses issued by the city. The sales of these medallions are said to be controlled and manipulated by a dozen taxicab brokers.

Any hardworking Joe who wants to earn his living by driving his own cab in New York must invest about forty-five thousand dollars in a medallion license, plus buy a cab and pay a year's insurance policy. Fleet operators must invest about twenty-five thousand dollars per medallion per cab. In order to pay the interest on this investment and amortize it in less than ten years, every cab must gross seventy-five hundred dollars a year, over and above its actual operating and maintenance cost. Of course not all try to amortize the investment, many owners simply figure on recouping and paying off the mortgages by selling the medallions to someone else in a few years. The cab has to be kept in operation twelve to twenty-four hours a day, and that means extra drivers must be hired.

How did this absurd and unique boondoggle come about?

Back in the early 1930s, the city sold the taxicab operating licenses, called medallions, for ten dollars to anyone who passed the police department screening test. The Great Depression caused a swarm of surplus cabs to jam the streets and in 1938 the number of medallions that could be outstanding was frozen at twelve thousand. The city then made the mistake of making them negotiable.

During and after World War II the price of these medallions soared fantastically. The prices got so high that some of the biggest fleet operators sold off their cabs, taking windfall profits and quit the business. As the city continued to grow, the twelve thousand limit on the number of medallions became absurdly inadequate. Legally, the city government could have abolished the limit or raised it at any time, but the medallions had become a Frankenstein's monster. If the city lifted the limit on the number, the price of medallions would sink. Banks and brokers who had lent many millions of dollars on them, would be left holding the bag. Lawyers for the taxicab operators, the taxicab drivers union and the taxi brokers threatened the city with huge lawsuits. Much political pressure was applied to stop the city from letting the medallion market collapse.

As the efficiency of law enforcement in New York declined, fleets of gypsy cabs that didn't have licenses appeared on the streets. Many were operated by fly-by-night characters with criminal backgrounds. But not all the illegal cabbies were disreputable by any means. The state government stepped in and licensed many of the gypsy cabs, although with somewhat limited rights to pick up fares. Meanwhile, the necessity for the medallion cab operators to earn so much extra revenue forced the fare so high that people began to cut down on cab riding dramatically.

Nobody seems to know just how many of the twelve thousand authorized medallions are actually in use, but someone owns every one of them. Those who own or control them are succeeding in keeping the price of medallions up in spite of the competition with the gypsy cabs, and in spite of high fares and declining use of cabs. Reporters who have investigated this huge boondoggle say it is manipulated through taxicab brokers but that the brokers are only front men. Those who make the profits and stand to lose the most if the medallion boondoggle were ended, are the banks and finance companies who lend the brokers operating capital.

A vastly bigger boondoggle of the same type that contributes much more to inflation and leads to crime is the liquor license racket in many states. Judges and politicians have been convicted of bribery in scandals over liquor licenses.

When the Prohibition Amendment was repealed in the early 1930s, a lot of well meaning officials, clergymen and others insisted that the number of retail liquor licenses issued in any community be strictly limited. Many persons at once saw a golden opportunity in this. These characters pointed out to the politicians that if they would make liquor licenses negotiable instruments, that would create a lovely harvest of thousand dollar bills for everyone who could get a finger in the pie. That this would grossly inflate the cost of investing in a bar or a first class restaurant wasn't so readily apparent in these depression years. But things went exactly as they did in the New York taxicab medallion boondoggle.

The only way to get a liquor license in many states is to buy a bar or restaurant that already has one. The market price of licenses depends partly on the retail potential of a given location but mainly on the scarcity of licenses and the amount of "squeeze" the local politicians can apply for approving the transfer. A typical example: A New Jersey seashore resort owner sold his liquor license because of ill health for fifty thousand dollars. Then his health improved and a banker offered to back him in opening a new ocean front restaurant. He began looking for a new liquor license. The cheapest one he could find cost *two hundred thousand dollars,* which included a small bar and grill which he had to buy and then close, in order to transfer the license.

Something like that happens everyday somewhere in the United States. It is one of the biggest reasons the restaurant business is so hazardous and restaurant prices are so inflated. Bankers and finance companies who make loans to finance the purchase of liquor licenses and even to finance the bribes for getting the licenses transferred, are big beneficiaries of the racket.

Another inflationary business phenomenon is the sale of trucking route certificates. Nowadays, it works almost like the New York taxicab medallion and the liquor license sales. In April 1977, Rep. Millicent Fenwick (R-New Jersey) and David Burnham, a reporter for *The New York Times,* accused the Interstate Commerce Commission of unfairly restricting the issuance of new trucking route certificates and thereby forcing anyone who wanted to go into the trucking business to buy up existing carriers who had had route licenses.

Burnham calculated that this ran the cost of some 360 license certificates up from $150,000 to $80 million in four years.

Rep. Fenwick and John W. Snow, former chairman of the National Highway Traffic Safety Administration, said this practice had virtually eliminated price competition in the trucking industry and had forced trucking freight rates up substantially. Mrs. Fenwick is introducing a bill to deal with the problem.

The American Trucking Association refused to comment directly on the issue, but did say that trucking is one of the most widely distributed of all business, with 12,000 of the 16,000 operators doing less than $500,000 a year in business.

Few government actions in our history, have accomplished so much good for large numbers of people as the food stamp program. Yet it too has been made a vehicle of boondoggling abuses. In spite of the cuts in the program made by the Ford Administartion, it was estimated that in the first half of 1976 about $110 million worth of food stamps were illegally or improperly obtained by persons who did not deserve them. Even if the figure is exagggerated, illegally issued food stamps obviously spread both inflation and corruption.

Student loans and the $5 billion a year paid out by the federal government in educational grants under the GI bill of rights have been another source of boondoggling that spurred inflation. Under the GI bill, an unmarried veteran going to college gets $292 a month in federal funds, a married veteran $347.

Stuart G. Feldman, who recently compiled a report on the actual workings of the program for the National League of Cities and the U.S. Conference of Mayors, said the greatest use of the program is in the western and southern states where tuition charges are low. He said the obvious reason for this is, in the states where tuition charges are high, the government payments leave little or nothing over for living expenses, so the veterans feel they cannot afford to take advantage of the program.

Guy H. McMichael III, counsel to the Senate subcommittee on veterans' affairs, said the program has been grossly abused. He said the worst abuse involves veterans who enrolled for the courses but never attended classes. They just collected their monthly checks while loafing or working on a job. McMichael said some colleges actively solicited GI students and didn't care a hoot whether or not they attended classes, so long as they paid their tuition bills. Some of these institutions created special curricular programs with easy and more or less meaningless courses for veterans, in order to get more of the program's gravy.

The General Accounting Office estimated the waste in the GI bill educational program for 1975 alone at $446 million in benefits improperly granted to veterans. Government officials estimate more of GI bill funds may have been wasted because some of the colleges don't even keep attendance records for GI bill students. These figures are inflationary with a capital I.

Valuable as the student loan program obviously has been to American society, it has resulted in a serious wave of bankruptcies by young graduates who don't want to spend years repaying the loans. Many of the bankruptcies are justified. The young graduate has made a vocational mistake and sees no other way of escaping a disastrous burden that will hamper him for years to come. But some of the bankruptcies are fraudulent and the government has obtained some convictions of graduates who concealed assets or made other false statements in bankrupting in order to avoid repaying student loans.

Some of the biggest boondoggles have involved various government housing and urban rehabilitation programs. Many of these have been marked by corrupt practices and scandalous behavior on the part of public officials, real estate developers, mortgage brokers and bankers that have cost the taxpayers many hundreds of millions of dollars.

Accelerated depreciation, a tax allowance designed to encourage building much-needed housing, has been turned into a boondoggle in nearly every part of the country. This activity has been most glaring in New York City as was noted in a *New York Times* editorial on January 29, 1977. After bitterly criticizing the shoddy design and construction of hundreds of expensive new apartment buildings put up in the city in recent years, the editorial said:

> Builders and real estate developers are not known for long vision. In fact, they see just as far as the tax books. The custom has been to take advantage of accelerated depreciation for ten years and then sell at the end of the bonanza period, with the next owner doing the same. The trip is down all the way. This doesn't help neighborhoods. It is hard to hold luxury garbage together; it deteriorates faster than old fashioned housing built to last. The falsely elegant becomes the obviously crummy. That is *real* accelerated depreciation, for which the city pays and pays.
>
> At present New Yorkers have no choice. The obvious and necessary alternative—the rehabilitation of sound older buildings with nine-foot ceilings, spacious rooms, solid hardware and vanished amenities—waits for willing capital investors who wait, in turn, for signs of active city commitment to neighborhood conservation. So far it is policy on paper only and the "luxury" rip-off continues.

The Justice Department recently hinted at the existence of a giant boondoggle that could hit the American people where it hurts most, in the weekly family food bill. The department issued a 585-page report sharply criticizing the Agriculture Department, the dairy farmers and dairy marketing co-operatives for using their nearly total control of the milk supply, to set prices well above free market levels.

Reporting on this, the magazine *Business Week* said it could be a harbinger of an ultimate full scale investigation into the possible abuse by many farm and food co-operatives of the privileges granted them under the Capper-Volstead Act back in 1922. This law granted the co-operatives exemption from the antitrust laws and in particular gave them the right to fix prices for their goods collectively.

Whether the activities of the co-operatives have played any greater role than those of the large commercial agribusiness corporations in the rising cost of living and consequent inflation, is a subject worthy of debate. An Iowa congressman, Edward Mezvinsky, was defeated in the 1976 election after he offered a bill to authorize a full-scale inquiry into what he called "the co-operatives' role in the skyrocketing prices of food." There isn't much chance of such an inquiry being held soon. Both President Carter and Agriculture Secretary Bergland are long time members of farm co-ops as are a considerable number of Senators and representatives.

The ten largest agribusiness corporations complain that the co-ops have an unfair tax advantage that gives them a potential opportunity to achieve control of the nation's food prices. These companies say their average effective overall federal tax rate is 32.2 per cent, while the ten largest co-ops pay an average of only 12.4 per cent.

What the American people should know is how much both sides battling for control of the nation's weekly food basket, are contributing to uncontrolled inflation by expensive activities that resemble boondoggles.

One of the more triumphant boondoggles of recent years was the purchase and remodeling of Yankee Stadium in New York by former Mayor John Lindsay. It started out to be a $29 million deal. The true cost still is not known for certain, but by the time the Yankee baseball team returned from Shea Stadium to the house that Ruth built, it was known that the city had poured at least $70 million into the venture.

A pipe dream may be as expensive as most boondoggles or more so, but often it is honest in its conception and even in its execution, which the boondoggle rarely is. Preston Tucker's marvelous new kind of automobile that somehow never got manufactured right after World War II is an example. Another was the late Howard Hughes "Spruce Goose" bomber. Another was the *Savannah,* the nuclear powered merchant ship that was a failure mainly for international political reasons. Too many countries would not allow her to dock in their harbors. The wasting of many millions of dollars in the attempt to build a nuclear powered airplane was an absurdity from the start. So have been many other military-industrial projects.

Gen. Joe Lawton Collins' tactical atomic bomb, to be fired from a cannon, was finally dismissed as a pipe dream. Some persons say that Rockwell International's controversial B-1 bomber is a $100 billion pipe dream, insisting there can be no suitable use for such a craft. The Navy keeps spending money on nuclear powered surface vessels, such as aircraft carriers. There is no clear evidence so far, that any aircraft carrier will ever be able to operate without a supporting fleet and if a ship cannot operate independently, like a long-range submarine, it obviously has no need for a nuclear propulsion plant.

From a strictly economic point of view, the entire space program on which we have spent so much money and of which we are so proud, could prove a pipe dream. It may never yield much in the way of real dividends, except some scientific and engineering knowledge that is already paying off—but will that knowledge really repay us for all that we have spent on the space program?

Housing programs have had their pipe dreams as well as their boondoggles. One example is the federal government's new community program. About $229 million in bonds were sold to finance the thirteen projects so far carried out in this program. 175 were planned. At the end of 1976 it seemed likely that at least $150 million of that would be lost. The projects were sponsored by local governments and private developers, beginning in 1970 under a plan controlled by the federal government's Community Development Corporation. After seven of the projects had defaulted on their obligations and the other six were in varying degrees of financial trouble, the program was sold to Congress as an alternative to suburban sprawl. The idea was to take maximum advantage of the opportunity plan comprehensively. The projects ranged from Cedar Riverside, a modest fifty-acre venture at Minneapolis, to Woodlands, an eighteen thousand-acre development at Houston that needed $100 million in startup money. A 6,000 acre project near Rochester, New York, called Gananda, was to achieve a population of fifty-five thousand. All were to be totally new communities, complete with ideal recreation and educational facilities and other public services and conveniences.

Reginald Stuart, an investigative reporter for *The New York Times,* said many of the other 175 new community projects still in the planning or construction stages, have fallen into so much financial trouble that their losses to taxpayers and private business might eventually run to $1 billion. The projects foundered on rising costs and high interest rates and the dissatisfaction of people who bought the homes. They were dissatisfied with the houses and the community environments. "Too many blacks" was a complaint frequently heard. The basic trouble seems to have been a combination of bad timing and over-grandiose planning, based on optimistic assumptions that failed.

It is rare to hear an expensive government program called a pipe dream by the cabinet officer responsible for administering it. Two successive secretaries of transportation, Claude Brinegar and William T. Coleman, tacitly, not explicitly, pinned that very label on Amtrak, the government-sponsored intercity passenger railway operating company.

Amtrak was conceived by President Nixon's first secretary of transportation, ex-Gov. John Volpe of Massachusetts. Volpe believed it would become a profit maker in a few years. Volpe's hope soon turned into a nightmare venture whose losses, borne by American taxpayers, have grown from $147.5 million in 1972 to $406 million in 1976. Shortly before leaving office, Secretary Coleman warned his successor, Congressman Brock Adams, that Amtrak could be costing the taxpayers $1 billion a year in the near future.

The chairman of Greyhound Corporation said Amtrak could cost more than that, because the subsidized competition it is posing for the buslines might bankrupt the highway passenger carriers. Amtrak officials retorted that the buslines are also subsidized by their getting use of the Interstate Highway System at low cost.

One way or another, subsidized travel is costing the American taxpayer an awful lot of money and that is contributing mightily to inflation.

Supporters claim the railroads overcharge Amtrak for the use of their trackage. The railroads main defense is that eventually they will likely be electrified with power produced by burning coal, and that then increasing use of passenger trains instead of buses and airplanes will help tremendously in solving the country's long-term energy problem.

A series of pipe dreams has involved small federal grants to develop new electric or steam-powered automobiles in order to reduce air pollution. The idea of the electric car is also aimed at substituting coal-generated electricity for gasoline. These grants, for the most part, were not given to groups with intensive automobile experience but to relatively inexperienced enthusiasts with some political pull.

The excuse for this was that the auto industry people, being firmly committed to gasoline and diesel power, would not make an honest effort to develop electric or steam vehicles, an idea which may have some factual basis.

None of the projects has accomplished anything to date in spite of the expenditure of some millions of dollars of tax monies. On the other hand, two private industrial corporations, Gould, Inc., the Chicago battery maker, and a joint venture of Gulf & Western Industries, Inc., with Occidental Petroleum Corporation, say they have made substantial progress toward developing new kinds of batteries to replace the conventional lead-acid battery and give an electric vehicle a chance to compete with a gasoline powered car for a large range of uses.

That the government-sponsored projects are largely pipe dreams is further indicated by the fact some of them call for design of a new car from the ground up instead of just a power train. The blunt truth is that any vehicle can be adapted to steam or electric power—if you can build an economical steam generator or an economical electric battery that will provide sufficient range and speed.

Of course, there is vast difference between a pipe dream and a necessary gamble. History will probably declare the space program to have been necessary, even for all its huge cost. We could not have refused the challenge. So it is with other challenges, such as the fast breeder reactor and nuclear fusion, costly as they will be. We cannot take the risk of not mastering those technologies and leaving the field to other nations, including the Soviet Union.

The large amounts being spent on cancer research are a necessary gamble, even if the odds are long. History does not show a high record of success for such massive research programs. The atomic energy breakthrough was an exception. Many, or most, of the great scientific discoveries have come from the intuitive genius of single individuals or small groups working in comparative obscurity on modest budgets. But we can't afford not to take the gamble on solving the problem of cancer.

It is well to remember that most boondoggles and pipe dreams paid for out of tax moneys are not all big deals, but there are an awful lot of them. They result from the constant pressure of academic and bureaucratic parasites who succeed in getting some pet scheme attached to an appropriation bill or a departmental budget. Many of the professed purposes of the grants are grotesquely absurd. But their real purpose is simple: to create artifical jobs. They also create artificial inflation.

6.

THE BLUNDER OF 1898

It is not possible to talk intelligently about the inflation of the American economy and the corruption of American life, without going back more than a century and surveying the consequences of several blunders by our forebears.

Nearly all our ancestors were guilty of at least approving many of the following errors, the consequences of which only the most sophisticated and farsighted persons could have foreseen. The first blunder was the uncritical acceptance of the doctrine of manifest destiny in the expansion of the frontier westward after the Civil War. It was indeed manifest that the exploding white populace, swelled by waves of immigrants from

Europe, would fill up the western territories. What should not have happened was the cynical violation of treaties with the Indians, the wholesale land frauds, the lawless violence, corruption and hypocrisy that accompanied the winning of the west. Young Theodore Roosevelt, Owen Wister and other authors who wrote in such glowing and romantic tones of the rapid pushing back of the frontier, ignored the harsh and corrupt reality. They and the politicians, clergy and educators gave the nation an utterly false picture of what was happening.

The majority of Americans in the last century averted their eyes from the crimes on the frontiers, just as the majority of Germans turned their eyes away from Hitler's crimes. The net result was the same: national corruption on a big scale and the planting of the seeds of hubris—unbridled arrogance. It would take these seeds forty to sixty years to germinate and grow into the noxious weeds that are threatening to choke us today.

This first blunder led to another and much greater mistake: the vastly popular Spanish-American war, a triumph of false idealism and romantic delusion. Out of our victory over Spain, won mainly by the Navy, in spite of some grotesque blundering and disgraceful savagery in the Philippines by the Army, grew nearly all our troubles of today.

But it was a "lovely" war that produced one of our authentic national heroes in the same Teddy Roosevelt, whose self-delusion had led him to write so much nonsense about the winning of the west. Because of his romantic role as a commander in Cuba of a regiment called the Rough Riders, which he had raised himself, Teddy was elected vice president, then became president when a lunatic anarchist assassinated William McKinley. The war was not so lovely for the thousands of soldiers who died of malaria and yellowjack in Florida cantonments while waiting to ship out to Cuba or the Philippines.

The ostensible purpose of the conflict was to free Cuba and the Philippines from Spanish tyranny, and to revenge the sinking of the battleship *Maine* while on a courtesy visit in Havana harbor. To this day no one really knows who blew up the *Maine* and no one ever has come up with a plausible reason why the Spaniards should have done so. The finger of suspicion has been pointed at various jingoist elements in the United States who stood to profit in one way or another as the result of a war with Spain.

The Republicans nowadays are fond of calling the Democrats the war party, but this romantic and easy little conflict with Spain which was to have such stupendous and delayed consequences was conceived and carried out by the GOP. Its architects were: McKinley and his secretary of state, John Hay; Senator Mark Hanna of Ohio; the real power behind McKinley, Roosevelt; publisher William Randolph Hearst, whose newspapers pressed the issue vigorously; and certain Wall Street interests.

The Democrats, then led by William Jennings Bryan, the populist from Nebraska, opposed the war, but rather feebly. Bryan's eloquence failed to dissuade thousands of young men from the South and other normally Democratic areas from volunteering. No draft was needed for this brief and popular war.

The triumph over Spain led to our assumption of colonial rule in Cuba, Puerto Rico and the Philippines. It was a betrayal of the principles of the Declaration of Independence, of the principles proclaimed by George Washington in his farewell address and of the principles of the Republican Party propounded by Abraham Lincoln.

However, it made the rest of the world sit up and take us far more seriously than ever before. Fortunately, that did not engender a wave of militarism at home. The Army was promptly reduced to normal size when hostilities ended. Roosevelt contented himself with fighting a pacifying operation against the Moros in the southern islands of the Philippines, and sending a battle fleet on a cruise around the globe to show our strength. For the most part we continued our posture of refusing to be involved in entangling alliances or other dangerous foreign adventures. Teddy did engineer a rebellion in Panama against Colombia, and built the Panama Canal. The action seemed justifiable at the time because of the frightful procrastination and venality of the feudal Colombian politicians. It was hailed as a notable political and engineering achievement (the Canal wasn't finished until Woodrow Wilson's time). Today the canal is strategically useless and a great political liability although of considerable commercial value. Our continued presence in Panama creates a focus of resentment against us throughout Latin America. We are justified in asking now if Roosevelt would have dreamed of seizing Panama the way he did if the war with Spain had not been fought and won.

Panama is the smallest evil result of the war with Spain. The really disastrous consequence was that it put us on a collision course with Japan, with whom we had maintained friendly relations for half a century. Our involvement in World War II probably would have been a one-ocean war in the Atlantic and Europe. It would likely have been followed by the same rapid disarmament and disengagement as our involvement in World War I, if we had not had to fight in the Pacific for our very survival.

After all we were allied with Russia against Hitler. Would Japan have forged an alliance with Germany if we had never penetrated so deeply into Asia? Would the war between China and Japan that started in the early 1930s have continued until it exploded into the Pearl Harbor attack, if we had never taken the Philippines from Spain? If we had not needed to fight Japan, how would we have become involved in Korea and Indo-China? How much less difficult might it have been to reach a reasonable accommodation with the Soviet Union if our differences with the communist bloc concerned only Europe and the Middle East?

In asking all these rhetorical questions we are also justified in asking what need would we now have for keeping three million persons in the armed forces (compared with three hundred thousand in the 1930s). What need would we have to maintain such a huge and costly military and defense establishment and so many bases around the world if we had never fought Spain?

Actually, the crime was not fighting and vanquishing Spain, but perverting the peace that followed the struggle from the espousal of Cuban and Philippine liberation into conquest and colonial aggrandizement. We "freed" Cuba but retained a huge naval base on her soil. We imposed on the Cubans the Platt Amendment, which gave Washington and American business a veto power over virtually every act of the Cuban government for forty years.

After crushing the Moros in the south Philippines we made the archipelago, first, a conquered territory, later a Commonwealth that in fact was a closely controlled dependency of the United States for forty-eight years. We still have large military bases in the Philippines and they are trying to make us pay dearly to let us keep them.

In doing all this we sowed the seeds of a whirlwind which inevitably struck and engulfed us. The two-ocean struggle of World War II drained us of our natural resources and forced the creation of a military-industrial juggernaut that we still cannot bring under control. It is this juggernaut that faces us with its recurring inflation, that every now and then gets completely out of control.

Our rule in Puerto Rico has not been without unforeseen difficulties. In drawing Puerto Rico out of Spain's economic sphere, we endeavored unsuccessfully to export to the crowded island our American standard of living. We could not give Puerto Rico the industrial base to support that standard. Hence, by the 1930s, the Puerto Ricans were mired in hopeless poverty and total disillusionment had succeeded their early enthusiasm for American rule. We did relatively much better in Puerto Rico in the long run than we did in Cuba or the Philippines. In the most recent elections on the island, the small independence party was soundly defeated. The Puerto Ricans appear to believe they eventually can pay their own way as the fifty-first state of the Union.

The island obviously never will be able to support its expanding population. It will have to continue exporting people to the other states of the country.

It is highly probable, in fact almost certain, that the United States ultimately would have become involved in the war against Hitler and Mussolini if the Japanese never had attacked us at Pearl Harbor. But the two-ocean war then and the later Korean and Vietnamese wars could have been avoided.

It was these that produced uncontrolled inflation and they were the logical consequences of the blunders by McKinley and Roosevelt after 1898.

7.

OUR INFLATIONARY TAX STRUCTURE

Economists and politicians commonly resort to raising taxes as a means of combatting inflation. The theory is that the increased taxes will sop up the excess money in circulation and thus have a braking effect on rising prices.

In the past when this idea was applied to individuals only, it frequently did halt inflation and simultaneously maintained the privileged classes in power, by taking away much of their gains from everyone who managed to profit enough by the inflation to move up a notch in the world. The tax increases never were enforced against the powerful as vigorously as against the common people. Difficult as it may be for some of us to realize now, most pre-industrial revolution societies accepted as basic the theory that taxes were to be collected mainly or entirely from the common people. The aristocracy enjoyed hereditary exemption from most taxes. The French Revolution was caused largely by the inability of the crown to persuade the shortsighted nobles to give up their tax exemptions; they had to give up their lives instead.

But in the modern world using taxation to curb inflation does not always work. It is not always possible because inflation is often accompanied by recession which demands tax relief. Also, the increased taxes are imposed on business as well as on individuals. Anything that increases the cost of doing business inevitably raises prices, unless the added cost is offset by great technological improvements that boost productivity substantially.

Corporate income and partnership business taxes, excise taxes and customs duties, sales and transaction taxes, business use and social security taxes and ordinary property taxes add up to a formidable component of the prices of everything.

What we must consider is whether the present American system, with its heavy reliance on the business income tax, is unduly inflationary and creates more temptation to corrupt practices than a more direct system of transaction taxes would.

When the federal income tax law went in effect in 1913 it applied mainly to individual incomes. The theory of Congress was that, eventually, all corporate profit became the private income of stockholders, partners, employees, etc., and would be taxed as such. The corporate tax rate then was only 1 per cent. This system worked well in the deflationary period from the end of World War I down to the Great Depression in 1930. Andrew Mellon, who was Secretary of the Treasury during much of that period, several times induced Congress to cut taxes. Some historians think the economic policies of the Coolidge Administration in the 1920s were too conservative and deflationary for the national good.

During the early depressed years of the Hoover Administration many corporations cut their cash outlays sharply because of bad business and began to retain large amounts of earnings. To President Franklin Delano Roosevelt and Congress it appeared that business, especially big business, was hoarding excessive amounts of money at the expense of the common people. FDR needed huge sums to finance his New Deal recovery program.

Inflating the dollar by doubling the official price of gold to thirty-five dollars an ounce did not raise nearly enough pump-priming money to get the stalled national economy moving. Personal income taxes of the well-to-do were raised, and for the first time the income of corporations and business partnerships was taxed heavily. Of course, this is double taxation—business income is taxed first against the business and again as private income of the stockholders.

Corporate income taxes soon became relatively more important than individual income taxes in over all national revenue. Before World War II accelerated this trend greatly, the tail was wagging the dog vigorously. Today, the personal tax is again more important than business income tax.

Many business men and some politicians and economists never have accepted as valid, the theory on which the business income tax rests. They say that in the long run it is self-defeating, has a stagnating effect on the economy and is insidiously inflationary. It limits productivity, favors big business at the expense of small business, limits competition and fosters a vast amount of waste and inefficiency. These are precisely the trends that encourage the development of uncontrolled inflation.

William Proxmire, the Democratic senator from Wisconsin, is chairman of the banking committee, and is certainly no tool of big business. On the contrary, he is one of business's more stinging critics on occasion, but Proxmire is also an ardent advocate of abolishing the corporate income tax. When the *Wall Street Journal* published an editorial on November 29, 1976, urging that the tax be abolished, Senator Proxmire wrote the editor of the big financial daily as follows—

> In your editorial you overlook the most useful benefit of such an abolition: the sharp reduction of corporate featherbedding.
>
> The corporate income tax gives corporate decision-makers a big incentive to waste corporate funds on everything from jet planes, theatre tickets and plush winter conventions in the Caribbean, to hiring unnecessary, often useless help.
>
> Why hold down corporate spending when Uncle Sam pays almost half of it? Abolish the 48 per cent corporate income

tax and you eliminate what may well be the biggest incentive for waste in the American tax system.

Your editorial also overlooks the fiercely anti-competitive effect of the corporate income tax. Thirty-five years ago two Harvard Business School scholars—Butters and Lintner—completed a study that showed that the mathematics of an approximately 50 per cent corporate income tax made it a devastating instrument in choking off the growth of the most efficient, and therefore, most rapidly growing new firms. The capital markets tend to be largely for the big boys. For the vast majority of fast growing firms, reinvestment of after-tax earnings is the best way to success and to challenging the established giants in the field. That 35-year old study showed that as of 1940 it was no accident that few new firms had risen to pose vigorous challenges in most industries. In 1976 the evidence is far more convincing.

So, abolition of the corporation income tax would sharply increase both productivity and competition in this country. . . . It also would give those of us in the Congress some respite from the corporate tax lobbyists. . . ."

If Senator Proxmire is right, the implications of his argument for solving our inflationary problem are great. An economy in which productivity can expand automatically without restraint is the best and perhaps the only surefire way to prevent uncontrolled inflation.

The degree to which the high corporate income tax provides incentives for business corruption is not hard to imagine. Just as Senator Proxmire observes that the tax destroys incentives for efficiency and innovation, so the tax can create incentives to evade it by dishonest accounting and to use it as an excuse for corrupt practices. "Why not rip off the stockholders a little? They're only losing a few pennies. Uncle Sam takes the biggest part of the loss." It's the identical kind of distorted thinking that enables the juvenile delinquent and the adult offender to rationalize every kind of crime by saying "Nobody gets hurt but the insurance companies and, brother, they deserve it, they've been screwing us all for years."

The attitude of top management toward standards of business ethics and business policy is equally distorted by the corporate income tax. In every quarter of every year, hundreds of big companies report net income (earnings) that are partly or totally fictitious because they do not represent profit earned out of operating revenues or investment income, but are only tax credits carried forward as a result of previous losses. This is not outrightly dishonest. Even a cursory reading of the earnings report reveals the true story; but it does foster a corrupt kind of economics, an acceptance of the idea that a loss can be a useful asset, and under our tax system it often is. Hundreds of businesses and properties are sold every year to companies that want them simply because they have accumulated losses that can be used to offset the profits of the purchasing company and reduce or even wipe out the federal income tax obligation. It is perfectly legal, and nearly all businessmen and accountants will insist it is also perfectly moral. But does it make for good national economic policy? And does it not have a distorting effect on business philosophy and ethics in general? It certainly costs the government money.

As with everything else, losses to create tax credits can be counterfeited by dishonest management people and they will be ignored by some accountants who will not probe too deeply if their fees are handsome enough. Remember, a CPA is only required to verify a tiny proportion of the data his business clients submit to him. The great mass of data the clients provide, the accountants perforce take on faith. We have had some truly astonishing examples in recent years, of big national accounting firms either being hoodwinked or deliberately looking the other way and ignoring scandalous swindles involving hundreds of millions of dollars.

The mere bite of the corporate income tax is bound to have a distorting effect on business policy and standards. The top managers of a corporation are saddled with a staggering burden of having to earn more than a dollar and a half to produce a dollar of true profit. Uncle Sam and the states where the company does business take the lion's share. Out of the remainder must come dividends on income stocks, on which shareholders will pay more income taxes. Even if dividends are small, Uncle Sam and the states will take a further toll from the individual shareholder in the form of capital gains taxes when he finally sells off some of his shares that have appreciated in value.

Perhaps it is ironic that Senator Proxmire's home state, Wisconsin, is one of the few in the Union that have experimented with the value added tax which usually is advanced as a logical alternative to the business income tax. France, the Soviet Union and many other nations rely on the value added tax as their primary source of revenue. In the Soviet Union and other communist countries, virtually all businesses are owned by the government, but the communist governments do not gamble on these enterprises making a profit, as our government gambles for primary revenue on the profitability of business.

The communist governments, like the French, collect revenue from business in value added taxes regardless of profitability. And it must be confessed that, although the communist countries all started after World War II with basic prices that were fearful by our standards, they all have managed to prevent runaway inflation.

The value added tax is a transaction tax levied at each step in the processing of materials and the manufacture of products. The tax is figured on the value added to the ultimate products at each step. Thus in a given year all businesses pay equal step taxes whether or not they are profitable. Does it really make sense for a company to pay no direct taxes to our federal government when it is doing a business of hundreds of millions of dollars simply because the year is not profitable?

Unlike the business income tax, the value added tax is not double taxation. Profits are taxed only once as personal income, after they are paid out in dividends or partnership fees.

The value added tax differs from a sales tax in that it is not levied directly on consumers. Nevertheless, labor economists and some academic economists insist it is only a hidden sales tax, hence is regressive and bears most heavily on the working classes. But this is highly debatable because in no free enterprise country using the value added tax is it relied on exclusively. Most of the countries also have individual income and capital gains taxes and perhaps small business income taxes.

The weight of the evidence seems to be that the value added tax raises revenue much faster than the business income tax. Also it is easier to collect; it encourages competition and capital formation and eliminates a host of domestic tax shelters. Above all, it encourages exports, which is certainly something the United States needs to do at present, considering the enormous trade deficit in 1976 and the huge deficit for the first quarter of 1977. The irony is, in spite of this, Senator Proxmire is opposed to a value added tax.

The value added tax encourages exports because it is not levied on goods intended from the start of processing and manufacture for export. It is relatively easy to rebate it on goods diverted to export from the domestic market. This greatly reduces unit costs of exported goods and makes them more competitive in world markets.

On the other hand it is extremely difficult to find a way to rebate taxes on the exported proportion of the production of a firm under the high corporate income tax system. It is rarely attempted. The only way the American company can reduce its taxes on exported goods is to make or assemble the products abroad and not bring home the profits from these operations. The rapid expansion of this trend after World War II caused Congress to pass laws to force repatriation of much of this profit so it could be taxed. But those laws made American goods so much less competitive in global markets that the Domestic International Sales Corporation (DISC) program was enacted to give the American manufacturer a better break. But the DISC program has aroused intense opposition by labor on the grounds that it encourages American firms to operate abroad instead of at home and thus exports jobs.

Recent history shows that countries that depend on the value added tax instead of a high corporate income tax can export more readily in competitive markets and their industries are under much less pressure to establish subsidiaries and branches to manufacture and assemble goods abroad than American firms are.

Up to now, the value added tax has aroused little enthusiasm in the United States but has curried much emotional opposition. There is too much fear that it would be manipulated to the advantage of the wealthy. The big corporations would again start hoarding excessive retained earnings, if the high corporate income tax were repealed. Nevertheless, Senator Proxmire's remarks about the inherently evil impact of the high business income tax should not be taken lightly.

Our present tax structure does limit competition, encourage waste and discourage productivity. It is bound to encourage serious inflation and discourage capital formation.

Our tax structure has been attacked as inflationary on other grounds. Professor Lawrence S. Seidman of the University of Pennsylvania's Wharton School has urged a tax incentive plan for both business and labor designed to control inflation by limiting wage increases. Seidman would give both employers and workers tax reductions, as a reward for holding wage boosts in any year down to a government prescribed norm. On the other hand, he would penalize income by tax surcharges for any company that raised wages more than the norm. The workers who got excessive increases would forfeit the tax cuts other workers got that year. This sounds like a difficult plan to execute and enforce.

Still another proposal for using tax reform to put an end to uncontrolled inflation was advanced in August, 1976, by the Advisory Commission on Intergovernmental Relations, a twenty-six member panel drawn from federal, state and local governments. The commission urged Congress to adopt a modified form of indexation adjustments on an annual basis to the personal income tax structure. These yearly adjustments would raise or lower the personal exemptions, deduction ceilings, and even the tax rates in accordance with the prevailing degree of inflation. But this clearly is not a plan to end uncontrolled inflation, it is a plan to accept it and try to live with it.

Indexation as a means of living under uncontrolled inflation has been used extensively in Brazil and other countries. Brazil has applied it to wages, salaries, prices, debts and virtually everything with the idea of making income and profit rise automatically at about the same rate as the inflation of money. Nearly all American businessmen and economists are dead against indexation for the obvious reason that it is a surrender to uncontrolled inflation and all the evils it spawns.

American businessmen who have lived and worked in Brazil in recent years say the indexation system works there only because the country is ruled by an authoritarian, but puritanical, military junta. They are emphatic in saying indexation would not work under the complicated democratic government in the United States but would only bring on chaos.

However, the commission made one telling point. It said inflation increases the government's income tax collections so rapidly that it provides a mighty temptation to congressmen and bureaucrats to spend extravagantly and thus aggravate the inflation.

Congress made an important change in 1976 in the tax laws regarding inheritances designed to prevent hoarding of assets in hereditary estates. For the first time it imposed capital gains taxes on inherited securities and other assets in addition to estate taxes. The capital gains tax does not have to be paid until the gain is realized by sale of the assets and is levied only on gains accumulated after December 31, 1976, because of the constitutional prohibition on retroactive taxes.

This change is certain to have far reaching consequences if it remains in effect. A Senate Budget Committee study favored the change on the grounds that it would improve the free flow of capital, but might it not have the opposite effect? Even if the new rule has the effect the Senate committee suggested, might that not prove inflationary by diminishing the incentive to long term investment of savings in growth securities?

Other economists who believe the corporate income tax should be abolished include Leonall Anderson of the Federal Reserve Bank of St. Louis, Dr. Martin S. Feldstein of Harvard University and Dr. Norman B. Ture, a consulting economist of Washington. They all proposed basically similar plans under which stockholders of corporations would be taxed not only on dividends, paid on their shares, but on a pro rata share of the corporation's retained earnings. Pension funds and charitable foundations would be exempt from this taxation.

This would eliminate the separate taxation of corporate profit and the double taxation of dividends. It would make a much larger portion of corporate earnings available for dividends and, since stockholders would be taxed on much of a company's retained earnings, it's logical to suppose they would demand bigger dividends and would vote management out of office if they didn't get them.

Another big problem of both the corporate and personal income tax under the present structure, is that they give such preferential treatment to debt investments as compared with equity investments. Interest payable on debt is deductible from taxable income both for individuals (although interest income is taxable) and for corporations while dividends are taxed twice. Does that really make sense in view of the fact that the country is facing a $600 billion capital shortage in the coming decade?

Robert M. Anthony, a professor at the Harvard Business School, has proposed adaptation of a method now being used in West Germany to ameliorate this problem. Anthony said, increasing the present small exclusion of dividends from taxable income would arouse too much emotional political opposition. Instead, he proposed "a corporate prime equity deduction," which would be instituted initially at 1 per cent of all pre-tax profit and rise year by year until it reached a maximum of 7 per cent or more. He claimed this would have the effect of partially equalizing the tax treatment of equity and debt investment.

There is another aspect of our tax system that is inflationary and also encourages crime and corruption. Legislators and politicians frequently tend to take a shortsighted and unbusinesslike view of excise tax rates.

They refuse to listen to warnings from the liquor and tobacco industries, for example, that very high tax rates are certain to run into the law of diminishing returns and produce less, rather than more revenue. When liquor and tobacco excise taxes are too high, the prices of legally sold liquors and cigarettes climb to inflationary levels and sales sometimes fall off. But the high taxes also result in a vast amount of moonshine distilling and cigarette bootlegging and in a brisk traffic in counterfeit revenue stamps.

An organization called the Citizens' Campaign Against Bootleg Cigarettes charged at a meeting early in May 1977 that New York City and N.Y. state were losing nearly $100 million a year in tax revenues on bootleg cigarettes. It urged that nine cents a pack be cut off the present tax level of twenty-three cents a pack in New York City.

The same group, headed by Alfred Donati, Jr., a state tax official, said organized crime probably had reaped about $427 million in profits on bootlegging cigarettes in the east alone between 1965 and 1975.

Sales taxes also can reach inflationary levels. The current New York City retail sales tax rate of eight per cent is clearly inflationary and is clearly damaging to retail trade in the metropolis. Many industries, the food business for example, operate on net profit rates, expressed as a percentage of sales, way below the tax rate.

But the politicians and other tax eaters don't care what effect their demands have on the rest of the people. They just keep on raising tax rates and increasing their pay and other government expenses, leaving the next administration to face the music. It's time to force them to change their tune. If we don't, they and the rest of us may be living at the poverty level by the end of the century.

8.

HOW MUCH INFLATION IS NORMAL?

The fact that the federal corporate income tax was so small until recent times, explains in some part why the United States had no uncontrolled inflation until after the Korean war.

However, since World War II we have had only two years of actual price declines, 1949 and 1954. Since 1968, the rate of price inflation has fallen below 6 per cent in only three years, 1971, 1972 and 1976. The peak rate of uncontrolled inflation was 12.2 per cent in 1974, and it obviously resulted from the cumulative impact of the big oil price boosts imposed by the Arab world late in 1973.

The inflation of World War II was high, but did not

get out of control. It dropped to an annual rate of 2.7 per cent in 1948 and then to the 1949 deflation of 1.8 per cent. But in 1950, the Korean war pushed the inflation rate up to 5.8 per cent and 5.9 per cent the next year. But the deflation that followed was precipitate with the rate of price increases falling to 0.9 per cent in 1952 and the price drop of 0.5 per cent in 1954.

From then until 1968, average annual price increases in the United States varied from 0.4 per cent in 1955 to 3.4 per cent in 1966. The significant fact is that there was no uniform upward trend. The course of prices followed the ups and downs of the law of supply and demand. Wage levels, of course, did not follow the law of supply and demand, they continued to rise, propelled by the power of the unions and the necessity of non-union employers to compete with union employers for workers.

In spite of wage increases, the course of inflation continued to be erratic. The annual level of price increases jumped from 0.4 per cent in 1955 to 2.9 per cent in 1956 and 3 per cent in 1957, then dropped to 1.8 per cent in the 1958 recession and continued to fall to 0.7 per cent in 1961. It fluctuated at between one and two per cent in the early 1960s, then jumped to 3.4 per cent in 1966 and to 6.1 per cent in 1969 as the war in Vietnam really began to be costly.

The winding down of the war brought the inflation rate back down to 3.4 per cent in 1972, then the oil price boosts sent it soaring again. These are not average figures for the years in question but the rate of inflation prevailing at the close of each year.

Contrary to some reports published at the time, the inflation rate actually dropped a little nearly every month in 1975 and 1976. The monthly preliminary reports of the Department of Commerce sometimes showed rising inflation but when all the figures finally were in, nearly every month showed an actual decline. The rate started off at 11.7 per cent per annum in January, 1975, and dropped to seven per cent by December. In 1976, the inflation rate fell from 6.8 per cent in January to 4.8 per cent in December. There were two small interruptions of this decline as the Consumer Price Index rose to 6.2 per cent in May from 6.1 per cent in April and to 5.6 per cent in August from 5.4 per cent in July.

A columnist writing in the *Wall Street Journal* concluded that "the outlook [to be derived from these figures] offers meager grounds for complacency." That's a sober conclusion and quite accurate. He also concluded that "there is no such thing as normal inflation" because inflation varies too much in different times and different places. Statistically, he is right. He is also right in saying that by no stretch of the imagination could the inflation the United States has experienced in the past quarter of a century be considered normal. The columnist, John O'Riley, was particularly incensed because he had read and heard from a lot of persons who ought to know better, that an annual inflation of six per cent is moderate. To columnist O'Riley's indignation I wish to shout a fervent "Amen."

O'Riley stopped just short of saying that a condition of no inflation is normal, and it's just as well that he did, because all history shows that some inflation, either continuous or intermittent, is the invariable experience of mankind. But the inflation must be kept under control and it must be held to a very low level. It would be climbing far out on the limb to suggest that I know for certain just how much inflation should be considered normal in the United States. The figures just related do suggest that the level probably should be well below three per cent a year and probably closer to 1.5 per cent.

We have little immediate hope as this is written, of getting our inflation rate below three per cent. Columnist O'Riley also made the point that high interest rates are inflation's handmaiden and we have seen the big banks' interest rate for prime business loans almost halved from 12 per cent in two years, which is a hopeful sign.

The principle that some inflation is normal must be accepted in the light of the historical trend of American wage levels. This trend shows beyond doubt, that union bargaining power is the determining factor in the rise and fall of wage levels. The alliance of labor and politicians has been sufficient for a long time now to offset much of the crude operation of the law of supply and demand. Labor cost is by far the biggest component of consumer prices.

Early economists, Adam Smith, David Ricardo and Thomas Robert Malthus, all taught that there is a natural price of labor—just above the subsistence level. Even Karl Marx accepted that, although he added to it the politically inflammatory idea of the surplus value of labor, for which the capitalist system does not compensate the worker. In the United States, our democratic political philosophy and the power of the unions has kept us from accepting the idea of a natural price of labor. American wages have nearly always risen in defiance of this idea, although there have been periods when wages fell. Economist Paul Douglas, who represented Illinois in the Senate, showed that real wages in the United States doubled between 1840 and 1890 and that real factory wages jumped 46 per cent from 1890 to 1926 without any inflation of the dollar occurring in foreign currency markets.

The 1920s produced hardly any wage increase, and the early 1930s brought a sharp decline. What happened was that normal wage and price inflation was interrupted in the 1920s and that helped to bring on the Great Depression. Indeed, it was the prime cause of the depression. Although most Americans believed the national economy was growing in the 1920s, it wasn't. The automobile; motion picture and radio broadcasting industries; the petroleum industry and road building were growing spectacularly. But the more basic industries such as steel, coal, the railroads, lumber, cotton and the other consumer product industries were largely stagnant because consumer buying power was not rising rapidly enough and credit was too restricted.

The only people making substantial profits were the privileged classes and those who were speculating in the stock market or commodity markets.

The farmers were going broke by the millions.

So we can draw the following conclusions:

Although the law of supply and demand operates fairly automatically in the labor market to determine how many persons shall be employed, it can no longer offset labor's united leverage power in setting wage levels.

Since wages are the biggest component of all prices, that means some degree of price inflation is inevitable and normal or else stagnation and depression will result.

Since wars and other catastrophic events will accelerate inflation from time to time, it follows that normal inflation must be held at the lowest possible rate.

Whenever inflation approaches three per cent a year at a time when there is no war or other continuing catastrophe, it is starting to get out of control.

The acceptable rate of peacetime inflation should be much less than three per cent a year. A word of caution: The view that the normal degree of inflation that can be tolerated safely is well below three per cent does not mean that price or wage increases larger than that should be tolerated. Our society and economy are much too complicated to be governed by any such simplistic idea.

Temporary fluctuations caused by weather, population shifts, and changes and improvements in technology all play too great roles in the matter.

Nor will the working man, having fought his way up over the centuries from manacled slavery, ever accept the idea that he does not have the right to continue the struggle to lift himself still higher at the expense of his contemporary betters. It is idle to talk about persuading him to tie his compensation to his level of productivity.

9.

INFLATION, SCARCITY AND JOBS

Before 1840 inflation was automatically and brutally corrected. If it resulted from frenzied speculation like Holland's tulip Bubble, or John Law's Mississippi Bubble in France, the inflationary structure eventually collapsed like a house of cards leaving a few persons immensely wealthier and hundreds of thousands bankrupted and ruined.

Wages were slashed ruthlessly. If the workers resisted, their leaders were hanged as an example and the ordinary workers were driven to their dawn-to-dusk toil by the lash and the bayonet. If the inflation resulted from scarcity caused by the scourge of one or more of St. John's apocalyptic horsemen, then the automatic correction was even more cruel. Hundreds of thousands starved to death in a few months. At first this aggravated the economic disaster because there were so few hands left to till the soil. But sooner or later an adequate harvest would be reached and then the reduced number of mouths to feed would convert the scarcity of food into a surplus and prices would come tumbling down.

In the modern world no such swift and merciless automatic rationalization is possible. The welfare state, the economic and political bargaining power of labor, rapid transportation and communications and the high state of economic sophistication accumulated in the last hundred years all intervene. The intervention of these forces has somewhat paradoxical consequences. It cushions the immediate impact of both inflation and deflation on individuals, but it greatly complicates and obstructs the correcting influence of the law of supply and demand.

The role modern financial sophistication plays in this intervention process is not widely understood, even though the sophistication developed over a considerable period of time. For example, few people realize that profit is a relatively new financial concept. Our forebears of less than two hundred years ago thought only in terms of gains on a deal, out of which operating and administrative costs and interest on capital had to be paid. Although these gains were sometimes enormous, our forefathers had not yet conceived the notion of net profit as something extra, a surplus to be reinvested as an expansion of capital.

To this day, there are a few economists who doubt

the legitimacy of such a concept, who believe the investor is entitled only to a return on his money and not to any growth of his capital. In point of fact, the degree to which the retained earnings and reinvested capital expand the value of the individual investor's holdings in a company is often problematic.

The rapid development of the concept of capital growth profit is an example of the kind of financial sophistication that helps complicate dealing with inflation in the modern world. The insistence of business entrepreneurs and their accountants on keeping prices high enough to return a profit large enough to keep their enterprises growing, prevents the kind of precipitate price declines that automatically cancelled inflationary waves in the past.

General accounting practices tend to conceal rather than reveal this kind of financial sophistication. The profit and loss statement of a company does distinguish between operating profit and capital gains on the sale of assets and other extraordinary profit, but the final residue out of gross income after all expenses of every kind have been deducted is simply called net income or profit. Amortization expenditures are duly specified, it is true, but when all is said and done, only an accounting expert could determine what proportion of this profit should properly be regarded as recompense for the company's operations and how much is really a return of capital for reinvestment.

Our income tax laws attempt in many abstruse ways to make this distinction. Income which we earn as wages, or dividends and interest from investments is taxed at one rate, and capital gains, which we make by selling or transferring securities or other property, are taxed at different rates and on different bases. The capital gains tax was not originally enacted as an anti-inflationary measure but to prevent too great concentration of wealth. Yet it is clear that, at least up to a point, the capital gains tax is a brake on inflation. It soaks up surplus wealth in inflationary periods.

The idea of the necessity of continuous growth profit made mincemeat out of the old fashioned idea that prices were fixed automatically by the law of supply and demand. As a matter of fact, prices have never been set mainly by supply and demand. They have always been administered in varying degree by brutal monopolistic practices backed by the law. The law was invariably framed to protect the gains of the processor and the large wholesale merchant, never to protect the consumer or the retailer. In ancient, medieval and recent times, legally proclaimed price scales always were minimum, not maximum, prices for the things ordinary folk had to buy. A baker in Elizabethan England, could be flogged or jailed for selling a loaf of bread for a farthing below the prescribed price, but the wholesaler could charge all the traffic would bear. The primary producers, such as the farmer and the miner, did not share in this price protection. They were forced to sell their grain, coal or ore at government fixed prices.

Legally prescribed wages were maximum, not minimum, for many centuries. A medieval employer could be branded with a hot iron or imprisoned for paying a worker a penny over the legal scale. He could make gifts to his workers, but only in food, shelter and clothing, never in money. He could give alms or make money gifts to anyone else.

Another aspect of modern financial sophistication that complicates the problem of dealing with inflation is "balance sheet competition." This has replaced the old fashioned concept of free and unrestricted competition, which never did operate so universally as some historians and orthodox economists would have us believe. The highly respected Harvard economist, John Kenneth Galbraith,* and David Bazelon,† have both explained that when modern business men talk about competition they frequently are talking about very strenuous non-competition.

What they really are competing at is to reduce inventories in order to create artificial scarcity so as to justify price boosts. This process reverses the dictum of the classical economists that competition holds prices down and curbs inflation.

The most inflationary aspect of today's financial sophistication has grown very slowly; this is the capitalization of practically everything on the basis of its maximum earning potential. This phenomenon was first observed in the 1890s by the great American economist Thorstein Veblen. Veblen discovered that business firms were capitalizing assets and carrying them on their books on the basis of their potential earning power rather than their intrinsic, functional or market value,

**In Defense of Business*, Harvard University Press, Cambridge, Mass.
†*The Paper Economy*, Random House, New York, 1959, 1964.

although market value tended to rise towards the potential earning value. Today this idea has been extended to the capitalization in the economy as a whole of the purchasing power of workers. Ironically, this can make the worker more valuable as a consumer than as a producer! It is the final proof of the ultimate futility of slavery and serfdom, the subjugation of the workers by slavery and serfdom put absolute limits on the expansibility and profitability of the economy. The only way to expand a slave economy was by conquest of new territory.

The modern worker may do more to make profits for business when he is shopping or loafing and consuming the things he has bought, than by toiling at his job. Clever modern entrepreneurs have learned how to expand the two to three hundred dollars of disposable income the modern worker has each month into several times that much in capitalized and recapitalized credit-debt instruments that earn paper profit for merchants, finance companies, banks and manufacturers.

As Bazelon remarks, this is quite an inflationary process. It puts all the emphasis on maintaining high prices and profits and comparatively little stress on increasing total productivity for the benefit of mankind. It is, in effect, a much wider application of the "conspicuous consumption" which Veblen condemned so vigorously in his famous work *The Theory of the Leisure Class.* Veblen denounced the conspicuous and ostentatious spending of the wealthy as pure waste.

John Law in the eighteenth century discovered that credit, which is just another word for debt, is almost infinitely expansible. So is paper capital and that has been recognized ever since Law's day. It works like this—

The common stock of a corporation with thirty million outstanding shares goes up one dollar in price. Instantaneously, that creates a potential of thirty million dollars in new borrowing power for the owners of the stock. The operative word is potential, and what counts is how skillfully and perhaps how unscrupulously the owners of the stock behave in maneuvering to acquire the added financial leverage foı a number of operations. But this thirty million dollars in new borrowing power, created by a mere one dollar rise in the stock, can set off a chain reaction that could create a totally new inflationary potential of $100 million in credit.

Every day, the prices of several hundred stocks and the prices of other assets such as bonds and real estate go up. This creates hundreds of millions of dollars worth of expanded credit-debt potential—opportunities for both borrowers and lenders to make huge profits.

Of course, the prices of lots of stocks and other assets go down every day, often more than go up, but *the contraction of debt-credit normally is a great deal slower than its expansion.* Therefore the inflationary impact of the debt-credit market is much more potent than its deflationary impact.

Finally, during much of the time since World War II, we have experienced a phenomenon called cost-push inflation. This results from increasing production costs and the overall push of the economy to provide full or nearly full employment. Shortening the work week and work day and other means of keeping more people working than are absolutely necessary in a given industry or company are examples of this.

If we reflect on it, we must conclude that this cost-push inflation is just Malthus's somber dictum that population growth always will stay a jump ahead of food production. If food production kept pace, the decrease in the workers' hours wouldn't cause prices to rise. Raising the standard of living causes a higher birth rate and a longer life span which then results in more workers than actually are needed. Instead of letting the surplus workers starve as our ancestors would have done, we inflate prices and money to keep most of them working.

A few years ago, a lot of people in America argued bluntly that we could never have full employment or anything near it, without having at the same time an unacceptable level of inflation. So it was argued that tolerating unemployment would prevent or reduce inflation. In those days inflation was running at only 3 to 4 per cent a year and unemployment at or under 4 per cent of the working force. The big increase in the global oil price late in 1973, produced both record inflation and record unemployment instead of full employment.

So we can deduce that the cost-push inflation created by the effort to maintain nearly full employment finally backfires. It prices hundreds of thousands of small businesses out of their markets throwing the proprietors and their workers into the ranks of the jobless. It makes most luxuries and many ordinary goods expensive. If something like the oil price boost occurs to aggravate the situation, even big companies are hit. They have to curtail production and lay off workers as did Detroit's automakers. Because of the unavailability of gasoline, industries such as the makers of recreational vehicles and operators of tourist attractions face temporary or permanent ruin.

Labor is not, as might be imagined, the chief beneficiary of cost-push inflation. Unless the inflation becomes so bad that profits are utterly wiped out, the chief beneficiaries of cost-push inflation are some of the people who scream about it the loudest, the banks, big insurance companies and various financial institutions that are able to make effective use of capitalized debt.

When the cost-push inflation reaches the point where the juggernaut no longer can be braked or even steered, then all these privileged institutions are hurt along with labor and the consumers.

Then they start screaming like stuck pigs.

10.

GETTING DOWN TO BRASS TACKS

If we are going to fight inflation, instead of just living with it in abject surrender, we have to get down to brass tacks and take some specific steps to strike a few blows for the cause.

Unfortunately, the attitude of most of the American people towards a personal fight against inflation is almost as belligerently defeatist as their refusal to believe in the grim reality of the long-range energy crisis. Very few persons are willing to think about making sacrifices for the cause.

Hardly anyone believes President Carter's proposed purchase taxes on big cars will stop people from buying them. Republican National Chairman Bill Brock said in

Chicago recently that the GOP will fight every effort of the president to tax either automobiles or motor fuel more severely.

Now, on the plain question of motor fuel, the future may find a way out. A workable fuel mixture that is only about half derived from petroleum, the rest from cheap replenishable alcohols and water, is a definite possibility. Although to produce and distribute the fuel would require a massive investment in technology and marketing.

But suppose that doesn't happen. Will the American people make the necessary sacrifices, or will Congress have to pass a coercive law forbidding the manufacture or use of cars that give fewer than thirty miles to the gallon of gasoline?

Will the majority of the population accept any sacrifices to end inflation as they accepted sacrifices to defeat Adolf Hitler and Benito Mussolini? Will they accept a return to the standards of hard work and thrift that enabled our ancestors to build this great country? Will they cling fatuously to the notion that by squandering billions on visionary technology, which yields only steadily diminishing returns, they can maintain a standard of living which we now can no longer afford? That is the real issue we all must face up to.

For those who choose the side of sanity and courageous sacrifice, here are a few suggestions:

Don't own an automobile unless you really cannot get along without one. If you use a car only once a month, it's cheaper to rent.

If you must keep a car, don't plan on trading it in

after three years. Plan to drive it eight to ten years. In order to do that you must follow the manufacturers maintenance schedule religiously. Also you must refrain from driving at unduly high speed; from "cowboy" starts; from overloading the car.

You might try using one of the new small four-cylinder cars that get thirty miles to the gallon. But don't pile the same load you would put in a Cadillac into the little baby and expect it to stand up. Bicycling is a wonderful way to combat inflation, and so are the little motorbikes that get more than a hundred miles to the gallon. A pair of them would be cheaper to buy and operate than a single car, but they are hardly to be recommended for those over sixty-five.

If you're a boating enthusiast, consider a smaller, slower boat that will give you about the same pleasure on a quarter of the outlay for fuel. Or, better still, consider a sailboat. Choose all your pleasures closer to home, and cultivate your neighbors. You may be surprised at how much money this will save.

The best way of all to fight inflation, is simply to refuse to pay inflated prices for anything. Food and shelter are the most difficult items on which to economize for the obvious reason that both the grocery business and urban rentals normally are low profit margin trades. Some families, whose disposable income has shrunk alarmingly because of inflation can relocate advantageously. You may not really need a house as big as the one you are occupying. Perhaps you can rent it out at a good price and live somewhere else more cheaply.

It still is possible to economize some on food but it is

more difficult than in the past. It is harder to get worthwhile discounts on case lots of canned goods at the supermarket than it used to be, or to buy large quantities of meats at discount prices to keep in the freezer. But the meat can be had at better prices if you put in special large orders. You can save fairly significant amounts by purchasing sugar, cereals and other staples, plus canned fruits and vegetables in the largest size containers offered.

Under today's conditions, the best way to save money on food is to modify your diet, and you may prolong your life in the process. Eat less meat and less sugar. Eat the cheaper cheeses and fruits and vegetables. Better grade canned fruits and vegetables are always cheaper than fresh produce and are about as nutritious. Avoid snack foods and things like "TV dinners." They may sound cheap but they are seldom flavorsome and their nutrition value per dollar may be low.

Consider the very high protein content of the many varieties of beans, lentils and the like. Properly prepared, they are wonderful and cheap variants for meats. And remember that gelatin desserts are among the cheapest as well as the most nutritious foods for both children and adults. Ice cream also is a good bargain. Remember that if you eat 20 per cent less, you will not only save 20 per cent more on your food bill but you will cut your daily calorie intake by an equal percentage. This will cut your doctor bills because your health is sure to improve.

That's getting in a real lick at inflation.

On nearly everything except food, shelter and health

care, you can fight inflation effectively, by simply refusing to pay inflated prices. Clothing is the easiest thing to save money on. Just make up your mind that nobody in the family is to buy any item of clothing unless it is on sale for at least one-third off regular prices. That means watching the newspaper ads and buying when things are offered for sale, not when you happen to want them. It also means turning your back resolutely on the latest fashions and dressing a little behind the times.

You can do the same with all kinds of housewares and household linens, sheets, towels and such. You can save even more sometimes on toiletries; if you keep your eyes open you may find soap that normally sells for thirty-five cents a bar on sale at four bars for something like seventy-five cents.

In buying anything at bargain prices, remember that it only pays to buy quality. A cheap suit that will only last a year isn't much of a bargain even at half price, but a handsome topcoat that will last five to six years may be an excellent bargain at a hundred and twenty-five dollars marked down from around a hundred and eighty-five.

I feel some hesitancy in presuming to advise feminine readers about buying clothing. The sober fact is that the gentler sex's reputation for skillful bargain-hunting is too often put to flight by their enthusiasm for the latest style and the newest designer colors. If the ladies really want to fight inflation, they'll have to curb these desires and choose garments that are a little more utilitarian.

Shoes, admittedly, are a problem for the inflation

fighter. Health depends so much on comfortable, well-made, well-fitting shoes. It's usually difficult to find good shoes on sale that will go with the rest of your clothes, but it's not hopeless. Most first class shoe stores have one or two sales a year and the discount outlet stores do offer surplus stocks of fine shoes at substantial bargains.

Giving up tobacco and cutting down on liquor are excellent ways to fight inflation. Not only will you save on immediate cash outlays, you may save some large doctors bills later on, by now averting nicotine poisoning and lessening the risk of the various ailments that are aggravated by too regular use of alcohol and/or tobacco.

Another way to combat inflation is to cut down on expensive tickets to sporting events, theatre and movies. Occasional tickets to the opera, symphony or ballet are well worth the investment, even at inflated prices. You can get a lot of sporting events and some good movies for free on TV. It must be admitted though, that the quality of dramatic entertainment on American television has been going downhill for several years.

If you are in business for yourself, you can fight inflation by watching expenses more closely than would be desirable in more normal times. Are so many of those business luncheons with sixty- to one-hundred-dollar tabs for four really necessary? Wouldn't a three-dollar phone call serve as well as a personal visit, which might cost fifteen to fifty dollars? Will that five-thousand-dollar color printing job on a report really impress customers and stockholders enough to justify the outlay?

"Schlock education" is another extravagance. The modern university has become a vast department store of courses for people of all ages. Many universities are simply out for the buck and no longer pretend to exist primarily to train adolescents for life. They still offer the hard-core courses in the sciences and the humanities which a real education depends on. Only a small portion of the faculties teach these courses. The rest of the professors teach the "schlock" courses, subjects supposed to be useful or "self-fulfilling" but are actually neither. They are just something to occupy people's time and take in checks at the bursar's cage.

Any one of these courses usually costs upwards of a hundred and seventy-five dollars a term, plus books. The schlock courses can be programmed to earn what real educators call "Mickey Mouse degrees." Charlatans equipped with these illusory degrees sometimes wangle their way into the faculties or administrative staffs of even good universities. Schlock education at the university level is just a very expensive waste.

Often it is an adolescent boondoggle at the expense of the student's parents. This "education" sends the "graduate" out to face life unequipped to be either a scholar, a professional man, a business man or even a well rounded human being. The student's parents may have squandered ten to twenty thousand dollars on the schlock education, and that contributes a lot to uncontrolled inflation.

So, to fight inflation, make sure that the money you spend on college courses goes for real, purposeful education, not counterfeit.

Universities are not the only purveyors of shoddy education. The flood of government money available for education in recent years caused a lot of trade and vocational schools to spring up. They offer schlock courses that are supposed to train people to get good jobs, but often are hopelessly out of date. Worse, some of these schools accept students who lack the aptitudes or secondary education needed to complete vocational courses.

Exercising great caution in using credit cards is also effective in combatting inflation. Remember that firms that accept credit cards have to raise their prices five to fifteen per cent to cover the credit card charge. Credit cards are also too big a temptation to extravagance. Debt piled up by credit card charges, just because the credit is easy to get, causes almost as much marital discord and puts about as many families on the financial rocks as unrestrained inflation itself.

I must concede that a lot of these suggestions in the standard articles and books on how to live with inflation also are helpful in combatting it. It makes sense to buy good common stocks, antiques, good paintings, income-producing real estate, diamonds, or other things likely to grow in value at least as fast as the inflation of money.

The "rip-off" psychology that has grown up in the United States in the past two decades is an enormous contributor to unrestrained inflation. We have already talked about some aspects of it in the chapters on the health cost scandal and boondoggles and pipe dreams. Basically the rip-off is a more personal thing. You are ripping off the boss and helping to inflate the economy when you take time off from your job that you are not entitled to, and are paid for the time.

Ripping off insurance companies by inflated accident and burglary claims runs to hundreds of millions of dollars every year. The resulting losses force rises in premium costs and threaten to reduce the availability of insurance for all of us. Inflated automobile claims are most common. A minor collision causes damage that can be repaired for about a hundred dollars. But as soon as the garage man learns an insurance company will have to pay, he works up an over-inflated bill and the owner of the car goes along because it is the line of least resistance. Besides, the garage man may offer him a kickback.

When personal injuries are involved, the claims may be inflated a great deal more. But the insurance company adjustors and lawyers are more vigilant today and put up a much better battle against being gouged by inflationary personal injury claims.

Some medical malpractice claims have the sound of rip-offs, so do many newer types of lawsuits growing out of the new Consumer Product Safety Act. A totally new social psychology about the financial liability of the medical practitioner and the manufacturers of all kinds of products has sprung up in recent years. In stark terms, this new psychology and the laws that have resulted from it say that somebody has to pay for everything untoward that happens to anyone; nothing is just misfortune any more. A natural corollary of that view is, if we seek a doctor's help and something goes wrong, it has to be the doctor's fault. It can't be our own fault or just fate. If an accident occurs while a child is playing with a toy, it has to be the toy manufacturer's fault for not printing on the box that if a kid pokes himself in the eye with the toy, it could cause serious injury. Some of the briefs filed in these new malpractice and consumer product safety lawsuits would have seemed utterly absurd only a few years ago. Many of the cases go to trial and result in jury awards for the claimants, while thousands are settled out of court to avoid the expense of a trial.

Shoplifting is another disgraceful rip-off that inflates the entire price structure. Much shoplifting is done by professionals, but more is done by ordinary people—housewives or employed men who simply want to live on a scale their pay checks will not support. Many have had their sense of right and wrong so blurred that they don't hesitate to pilfer hundreds of dollars worth of merchandise every year from the stores where they shop.

It is not easy to calculate exactly how much the rip-off psychology contributes to runaway inflation, but the National Retail Merchants Association has estimated for some years now that shoplifting adds at least five per cent and possibly ten per cent to the general retail price level. Each and every one of us can fight inflation by refusing to tolerate the rip-off psychology.

Ripping off insurance companies and other businesses is also carried out by professional criminals and politically oriented groups raising money to finance large scale terrorist activities. Of course, it is useless to appeal to such people to cease and desist. However, it is imperative to make an urgent appeal to the managements of the insurance companies and other businesses that are the targets of these inflationary crimes. They must be a lot more vigilant in preventing these rip-offs and a great deal more diligent in prosecuting the offenders when they are caught.

Faked automobile theft claims and faked burglary claims are a growing scandal. The police of several large cities say a growing proportion of the automobiles, jewelry and other valuables on which large theft claims are being collected are non-existent. If they do exist, they were merely "borrowed" for inspection by the insurance agent when the policy was written. They were then reported stolen and a big claim was collected. If the insured articles are really owned by the policyholder, he may have sold them to a fence who then helped him fake the burglary and collect the insurance claims.

On February 20, 1977, *The New York Times* described the operation of a rip-off of insurance companies amounting to at least $5 million by a ring of Arab students in California. They were funnelling the money they gained in this way to the Palestinian Liberation Organization. The students were provided with funds to buy automobiles. The autos were insured, then turned over to the PLO, shipped to the Middle East, and sold at five or six times their cost in California. Meanwhile, the Arab students collected the insurance on the "stolen" cars. Some of the students operated under several aliases and worked this racket with several cars simultaneously. The article said the same Arab ring also collected large sums from California insurance companies for faked burglaries and faked personal injury claims.

This racket is not confined to California. The reason it works so well is simple. Insurance executives and adjustors are too lax in checking out applicants for policies and in investigating claims before paying them. If everybody in the property and casualty insurance business did his job conscientiously, an inflationary rip-off such as this would be discovered and squelched rather quickly.

Commercial bribery is another contribution to uncontrolled inflation. All of us can do something about it by resolving to turn our backs on it firmly. The news media have been loud in the past two years on recounting the illegal and improper payments American companies made in foreign countries in order to do business. These payments ran to many millions of dollars, but they are a drop in the bucket compared with the flood of ordinary bribes and kickbacks paid out in domestic business by dishonest executives and salesmen to crooked purchasing agents.

Some well-informed experts have calculated that a company that pays bribes and kickbacks must, on the average, sell an additional twenty dollars worth of goods or services to cover each dollar paid out in the bribes and kickbacks. Likewise, a company whose executives are taking bribes and kickbacks from suppliers must rack up about twenty dollars worth of extra sales to offset each dollar of higher prices it is paying suppliers because of the sums its executives are pocketing.

Also, it is incumbent on all of us to become better

informed about our nation's foreign relations and about the true nature of our vastly expensive military-naval establishment and defense industry. We never will be able to conquer uncontrolled inflation without putting the generals and admirals back under firm civilian control and doing the same to the entrenched defense contractors. It is necessary to do this in order to bring an ultimate end to the cold war.

There are no easy paths to this goal and no way of reaching final agreements with the Russians, the mainland Chinese and the Arabs overnight. Nor can we cut our defense spending precipitately. It should be self-evident that a much better job can be done than was accomplished by either the Johnson or the Nixon-Ford administrations. We can save a lot of money and deal uncontrolled inflation a hard blow in the process.

Another effective thing we could do to fight inflation would be to solve the narcotics problem. The illegal narcotics trade drains several billion dollars a year out of the pockets of Americans. The size of the traffic is somewhat exaggerated in the public mind, but its cost in human suffering and nonproductivity is not exaggerated. Young people of both sexes are the victims and members of the racial minorities are particularly vulnerable to being enchained by narcotics.

The narcotics traffic often is described as the creation of the Mafia, which certainly controls it. But the Mafia did not create it. It was created by high-minded naiveté, the same kind of naiveté that created the profitable bootleg liquor traffic in the 1920s. If you go to the public library and examine the files of popular newspapers and magazines for the years around 1910, you may be astonished to find advertisements offering Americans cold cures containing the "wonder drug heroin" and other opium derivatives sold freely over the counter without a prescription at one time for as little as twenty-five cents a bottle. That means that in those days an addict could get a "fix" for less than a quarter. Today a junkie has to pay a dope peddler five to ten dollars for a "nickel bag" fix. That's a degree of inflation to boggle the mind and it all goes into the pockets of criminals.

The national anti-narcotic law was pushed through Congress by an earnest young lawmaker from Mississippi named Pat Harrison. At the time there were an estimated 1.25 million addicts in the United States. They were addicted either to cocaine or to morphine sulfate, the common hospital painkiller. The morphine habit is relatively easy for the individual to break as compared with heroin, which is many times as addictive and many times as dangerous as morphine.

To do Pat Harrison's memory justice, his new law worked very well for thirty years, but Harrison had gone one step too far. By forbidding physicians to prescribe narcotics for addicts, he had planted a time bomb. The law ultimately became an ideal vehicle for exploitation by the kind of criminals who never operate on profit turnovers of less than one thousand per cent and often get fifteen thousand per cent. The criminals were slow to take advantage of Harrison's law because the bottleg liquor trade and various extortion rackets were such gold mines in the 1920s and early 1930s.

But after World War II, the mobs began pushing heroin, cocaine and other drugs with a vengeance. Their pushers hooked kids as young as ten years old on the drugs, forcing them into crime or prostitution to support their habits.

A mildly narcotic leaf plant, marijuana, which had been in use at least two centuries, also was pushed by the criminals. A fantastically popular cult was built up around its use by the young. Marijuana appeals to persons a little too smart to get hooked on heroin or cocaine, but who are attracted by the "drug scene." This scene soon embraced other drugs such as the amphetamines and the hallucinogenic compounds such as LSD.

Its huge profitability has clearly made the illegal narcotics traffic an inflationary force in itself. When we consider the added cost of the murders and other crimes committed in the drug traffic and the cost of shattered lives of addicts, the inflationary impact is greatly magnified.

Much of that impact could be ended by the simple expedient of replacing Harrison's law, which still is on the statute books, with a more sensible law. Physicians should be allowed to prescribe narcotics for addicts, thus taking away the big profits that criminals reap from the trade. Criminals cannot operate without the huge profit. Marijuana could be decriminalized. It is harmful to the human system but not much more so than tobacco and possibly less harmful than alcohol.

Giving personal advice to poor people on how to combat inflation requires a bit of gall. Complaining that the cost of maintaining some millions of people on welfare payments is a severe inflationary burden has a frightfully hollow and callous ring to a man in his forties who has been out of work two years and is told by one employer after another that he can't hire him because he is overqualified. It has an equally cruel sound to young blacks and Hispanics who are unqualified because they couldn't overcome almost hopeless odds in the home or at school.

Telling immigrants from the backwaters of the world that having many children is bad because it fuels inflation flies in the face of all their traditions and instincts. These persons take it for granted that they will be dependent on their children in their old age, so they want to have plenty of them.

The poor already know that uncontrolled inflation runs up the prices of everything they must buy. This makes their life more miserable, but if we are to persuade them to vote for politicians and for measures that will curb inflation, we have got to convince them that ending uncontrolled inflation also will help them find work and dignity, and that's a tall order. What we need to demonstrate to the poor, in order to win their support, is that reducing poverty depends on increasing productivity, just as ending runaway inflation depends on increased productivity.

The votes of the poor are essential to winning the fight against uncontrolled inflation and to get them we must convince them we are on their side. Unfortunately, in spite of the fact that most politicians champion the cause of the poor clamorously, some sociologists say the great mass of the American people not only show little concern for their welfare but actually are hostile toward the poor. They say the well-to-do and even the working classes look on the chronically poor as a great embarrassment; a living refutation of the American dream; a denial of all our cherished national beliefs.

That's hardly something new in the world. Most ancient religions and ancient social systems despised the poor. They taught that poor people were those who had displeased the gods and therefore deserved their harsh conditions. On the other hand, it was accepted in these faiths and social systems that the rich and the elite were those who had served the gods well and earned their favor and their privileges. The poor were fit only to be slaves and outcasts. Far from seeking to help the poor, those who were fortunate were abjured to have nothing to do with them lest they offend the gods who had punished the miserable wretches. Judaism was the first religion to challenge this cruel idea, then the Christian apostles, following the teaching of Jesus, attacked it boldly.

If the sociologists are right, we Americans are in danger of falling into this ancient and callous philosophy. This philosophy helped wreck so many past societies. If we do that, the poor will eventually become desperate enough to resort to destructive terrorism on a large scale, as they always have in the past.

The consumer movement is raising questions that have a bearing on what the individual can do about inflation. Consumer advocates have been pushing boycotts of foods such as sugar, coffee and concentrated frozen orange juice that go up inordinately in price. In the case of the big rise in sugar prices in 1976, the consumerists were joined by some supermarket chains. The markets management said the price rise had exceeded all justification and they urged housewives not to buy sugar until the price went down, which it ultimately did.

The concentrated frozen orange juice price surge, was caused by the bitter weather of January and February, 1977. The high prices of coffee were caused by two successive years of freezes in the coffee growing areas of Latin America. Some consumer groups charged that prices went up much more than warranted by the damage. Whatever the truth, the result was higher prices to consumers and windfall profits for processors and merchants.

Several congressmen saw the prolonged rise of coffee prices as a golden opportunity to make political hay by charging that the coffee shortage was a myth and rip-off.

Little or no evidence was advanced to show conspiracy or a real rip-off, but an interesting question was raised: To what extent are processors and wholesalers or retailers entitled to windfall profits on stocks on hand, when natural disasters cause a shortage or threaten a shortage of a commodity?

Historically, the right of merchants to "charge all the traffic will bear" under such circumstances had never been challenged before. Wholesalers and retailers claim they are entitled to the windfall profits because they have to take losses on inventories when prices go down. But in the present inflationary climate, price rises are so frequent and so seldom are reversed that they arouse deep resentment. Therefore, the consumerists are demanding: Have wholesalers and retailers got any right to raise prices before they are forced to buy new stock at higher prices? In other words, no windfall profit.

If the public supports the consumerists in this challenge, another blow will be dealt at inflation.

11.

LET'S RETURN TO THE WORK ETHIC

In one of my previous books* I had chapters entitled "An Ounce of Prevention" and "Living With Inflation." These discussed the problems of cost-push inflation in the peak years of the Vietnam war when Lyndon Johnson was president. The inflation was then out of control, but did not approach the 12 per cent level it reached after the energy crisis of 1973. The chapter on prevention argued thus:

> If we abdicate our responsibility as citizens to the politicians and to the business and financial community, the task of sensible economic management then will become much more

**Inflation: Everyone's Problem*, Citadel Press, New York, 1968.

> difficult. Although a hundred years ago it was fashionable among scholars to contend that government by an aristocracy or a powerful elite was more likely to be enlightened and efficient than government by the democratic mob, all history shows the exact opposite to be true. Very little social or technical progress was ever made under feudal governments. Democratic regimes, whether based on free enterprise or socialist economics, have produced vastly more progress.

This chapter also pleaded for continued devotion to an old American ideal, a full day's work for a full day's pay. The chapter on living with inflation dealt with the eternal desirability of taking a thrifty and practical attitude in coping with the problem of prices going up faster than the weekly pay check can accommodate.

We faced much the same dilemma then as now. The basic problem for an industrialized nation in dealing with spiraling prices is to strike a balance between the need to keep the inevitable minimal amount of inflation from becoming, first, an immoderate rate of cost-push inflation to create jobs, and then bursting into uncontrolled inflation.

A journalist friend told me of an example that is a microcosm of how failure to face up to this dilemma can have very disastrous consequences. He said when he first began working in New York in the mid-1930s, the newspaper printers' union's basic wage scale was seventy-four dollars for a five-day week. Top scale editorial workers, who were just starting to unionize, were getting forty-five to sixty dollars for a six-day week.

In the next thirty years, a period punctuated by strikes of both the Typographical Union and the editorial and commercial workers Newspaper Guild, the two unions followed highly divergent policies. The printers, who long had enjoyed the benefits of feather bedding craft rules, negotiated primarily to keep all their members working rather than for more money. They adamantly resisted every proposal to introduce new labor-saving machinery or to do away with the feather bedding.

The Newspaper Guild also sought to expand employment by reducing the workers' hours. It negotiated every year for higher salaries and made no effort to prevent the introduction of electronic communications equipment and no effort to force the newspapers to keep unneeded workers.

What was the result?

The printers, by doggedly forcing the publishers to use outmoded equipment and to keep extra workers, soon found their ability to bargain for improved wages had vastly diminished because their productivity had declined. The editorial workers, whose pay scales had lagged behind those of the printers for half a century, now not only caught up, but the top Guild scale ultimately exceeded the top printers' scale by a hundred dollars a week.

New York lost seven dailies during those years. My friend says they died for a variety of reasons: the competition of television for advertising and audience; the movement of population from the city to the suburbs; the rising cost of newsprint; the heavy cost of trucking evening papers through dense traffic and particularly the refusal of the mechanical unions to accept automation until it was too late.

The death of the seven dailies caused both the mechanical craft workers and the editorial and commercial workers to lose their jobs. But higher wages had attracted better educated people in the editorial and commercial departments and they were better able to find other jobs than the displaced mechanical craftsmen. The editorial people went into broadcasting, book and magazine publishing, advertising, public relations and teaching.

Putting too much emphasis on full employment and thereby bringing on a boom-and-bust cycle could have this same effect on a much wider scale.

It used to be believed that pensioners and salaried people were the main sufferers from inflation. Also that speculators and many businessmen prospered because inflation brought higher profit margins. That idea was eventually succeeded by the view that "everyone loses by inflation." Professor George L. Bach of Stanford University, whom economists regard as well informed on the subject, says not all lose by inflation. He says that in the inflationary periods in the United States from 1950 through 1975, things went quite differently than in earlier inflationary periods in Europe.

Professor Bach says businessmen have been the big losers from the inflation of the past quarter century. Corporate profits, he says, lost eight per cent of their share of the national income, while labor gained 10.7 per cent and pensioners gained eight per cent. The banks increased their slice of the pie by almost six per cent and landlords by 2.4 per cent. Taxes grabbed off an additional 7.5 per cent of the Gross National Product as a result of inflation, according to Professor Bach's reckoning. Professor Bach adds that the increases in the share in the national income of the banks and the tax collectors have had a quite damaging effect on national economic growth because that much money is taken away from the supply of the investment capital that creates productive jobs.

So we come down to the fact that holding inflation to the minimum inevitable level is an extremely complex problem. It calls for determined and sophisticated measures by government and business leaders and dedicated response by the people. Nevertheless, the whole problem boils down to one word—productivity. *A nation whose economic productivity continues to rise at a healthy rate will be able to keep inflation under control.*

"Buy American" slogans can't do very much to check the flood of imports that have produced the current trade deficit. Many of the imports are vitally needed. A rise in domestic productivity could bolster exports and turn the tide.

Higher tariffs won't do too much good either, except on a highly selective basis; it is too easy for other nations to retaliate by raising tariffs against American goods. But, again, rising productivity can make domestic goods much more competitive with imports.

Increasing productivity is the only way we can reverse or even check the upward spiral that has priced new homes and new automobiles and many other products out of the reach of many American workers. We have tried price and wage controls and have discovered they only work moderately well under the stern discipline of wartime. In time of peace or even during such conflicts as the Korean and Vietnamese wars, they are too difficult to enforce.

The trouble is, few persons have a clear idea of what productivity means and how they personally should contribute to it. The economists define productivity as the unit output measured in man hours in an industry or company in relation to the capital invested. But that definition doesn't tell the ordinary office or factory worker how to measure his or her productivity, it's too impersonal, too unrelated to what the individual actually does on the job. One worker sits at a console all day and monitors dials at stated intervals. The rest of the time he is free to read, listen to music or flirt with the female help. How does he measure his personal productivity? For the salesman who has a quota to meet, the assembly worker who must keep up with a production line or the teacher who must pound so much math or English into the heads of thirty kids, achieving measurement is easier.

When you think it over you realize there is only one satisfactory answer for most of us, from the company president down to the humblest maintenance man or clerk.

Personal productivity depends on tackling your job conscientiously and intelligently all the time.

If everyone in the country does that, industrial productivity and national productivity are bound to rise steadily. That will make uncontrolled inflation impossible. Of course it isn't possible for all of us to measure the degree of earnestness and good judgment with which we apply ourselves to our jobs. But we know when we are goofing off and not really trying.

The key element of productivity is the work ethic. The voluntary work ethic is the cornerstone of democratic civilization. The only alternatives to following it are the various forms of authoritarian rule which inevitably sink into totalitarian societies—ranging from feudal serfdom to Marxism. The principle seems axiomatic, yet a wide challenge has been hurled at the work ethic since World War II. In America it began with the beatniks of the 1950s and proliferated into many kaleidoscopic movements of restless people fleeing traditional morality and responsibility. The hippies and "flower children" and some of the new communal religious cults disdained the Judeo-Christian work ethic.

Perhaps the most insidious and dangerous threat to the work ethic is expressed by Americans who have been living in Europe. They parrot a comment made years ago by some writer or other who said "Americans live to work but Europeans work to live," which, he said, was a much more civilized attitude.

Nothing could be farther from the truth.

The slogan-like phrase "working to live" implies that at some point work ceases and one just exists in idle freedom like the animals and the birds. For a human being endowed with a thinking brain instead of the reactive brain of an animal that is not possible without falling into stagnation and degeneracy. One cannot truly live without working. Even if one does not pursue a gainful occupation because he or she already has enough money, work must be continued if life is not to become stale and hard to endure. No matter what interest one acquires: music, art, literature, a scientific hobby, physical sports, or romancing, it is necessary to work at it hard to achieve any degree of satisfaction. Many people who retire discover that being retired is a rather strenuous occupation.

There is only one escape from the work ethic, both for the individual and for an entire society. But that escape usually turns out to be as bad as Faust's bargain with Mephistopheles. The alternative is total surrender to hedonism, the doctrine that pleasure is the only goal in life. But for centuries the sober weight of evidence is that abandonment to pleasure can lead only to boredom and ultimately to frustration, stagnation and disintegration of personality with the resulting decline of all one's talents and powers.

Nevertheless, an astonishing number of persons who should know better, go about prattling the nonsense that we must work to live instead of living to work. You hear it from university professors, from clergymen, from labor leaders and politicians, from writers and a host of muddleheaded characters. They range from dropout juvenile delinquents to septuagenarians, from bums begging on the streets to smartly dressed folk at cocktail parties.

They're all wrong. You can't work to live—you have to live to work or sink into personal failure. If Americans stop living to work, this country will sink into failure as so much of the rest of the world already has.

One of the most recent testimonies to the value of

the work ethic came in a speech by the dissident Russian writer, Andrei Amalrik, on the occasion of his receiving the 1976 human rights award of the International League of Human Rights. Among other things, Amalrik said in part:

> Instead of giving $1,000 to each poor person, as Senator McGovern proposed during his campaign, it is necessary to provide assurance that a person can earn money for himself, to provide education and a job, and to make people aware of themselves as individuals.
>
> The view which opposes one category of rights to the other is historically mistaken because wherever individual liberty has been sacrificed to achieve social and economic goals, social rights have suffered in comparison with their development in free countries. . . .
>
> I believe that the success of Marxism can be explained by the fact that classic liberalism, the ideology which has shaped contemporary western society, is experiencing a crisis, perhaps a fatal crisis. . . .
>
> The ideology of liberalism changed the world for the better. But it failed to answer many questions. In effect, the liberal ideology throws a man into the sea and says: Sink or swim. The liberal credo is: Leave me alone and I will leave you alone.
>
> And this credo is the apparent cause for the crisis of liberalism. People don't want to be left alone. They want others to care about them. They want something to be asked of them. . . .
>
> And this is where Marxism enters the scene.
>
> Marxism has placed its stake on force, which Marx called the midwife of history. Even though this midwife perpetually delivers monsters and not normal children, Marxists never tire of promising that the next child will be a splendid one.

I don't believe the Marxists. Many don't believe them, but they enjoy a great advantage. No matter how bad their prescriptions may be, they understand that the world is inevitably changing and they want to grasp this change and direct it.

What do liberals want? What do they propose? To preserve what exists, to turn the clock back. To "adjust to reality"—that means, in effect, endless concessions to communism in order to preserve a tranquil life for another year . . .

I believe that everyone who values freedom is confronted by the problem of creating a new ideology which will transcend both liberalism and communism and make its central issue the indivisible rights of man.

Some people thirst for revolution. Others fear it. But which revolution is meant?

I want to contrast two revolutions. The revolution which occurred in your country two centuries ago and the revolution which occurred in my country little more than half a century ago. During the past two hundred years, people from all corners of the world have flocked to your country. Almost as many have fled from my country during the past sixty years.

No better comparison of these revolutions is needed than their attitude toward people and people's attitude towards them. I am for revolution, but I am for a humanitarian revolution.

And now, in appealing to you, I am appealing to the American revolutionary spirit. . . .

In other words, as I see this dissident Russian's comments, it is the voluntary work ethic that we in this nation should continue to cherish and work at until death do us part.

However, my immediate concern with restoring the work ethic is its effect on personal productivity and ultimately on national productivity.

It is no accident that the two countries where the work ethic was first challenged and where its prestige has fallen most are Britain and Italy. In both countries the currency has been so whittled by inflation and devaluations, that it is barely passable on the world's money markets. Britain and Italy are in such dire economic straits that there isn't a statesman or an economist in the free world who sees any chance of saving them from prolonged poverty.

We have the evidence of numerous American observers, and of the English themselves, that the outstanding cause of their difficulties is the "take it easy" attitude on the part of a large sector of the country's population. There's also a rigid unwillingness by British labor to cooperate in getting costs down which could make British products competitive again in world markets.

The English have rightly been described as "the toughest, stubbornnest people in the world." But in recent years their stubbornness more often has seemed like bullheaded complacency in the face of imminent ruin. They simply can't "put it together" and work hard to overcome the great setbacks caused by the loss of their overseas empire and the big reason is that too many Britons refuse to live to work.

The appalling drops in British and Italian productivity have been more quantitative than qualitative. The prestige of many of their products is still high, but the inefficiency of their industrial organization is mind boggling. They cannot sell on world markets except by periodically devaluing their currencies to get prices down.

If we Americans fail to restore the work ethic and maintain it, we could sink into the same stubborn complacency and bring on new, more violently unrestrained, inflation.

Robert Half, head of one of the country's larger national personnel consulting agencies, has estimated that the "take it easy" attitude, which he called "the theft of time," costs American business and other institutions $70 billion a year. If Mr. Half is only half right, that's still one whale of a contribution to inflation. But Half says the take it easy attitude also contributes to corruption because many workers use the stolen time and their employers' telephones to sell mutual fund shares, real estate or encyclopedias. As was aptly said many, many years before my time, "Steal my money, you steal trash . . . steal part of my time, you steal part of my life."

Nowhere is a return to the work ethic more needed than in government services. Since the inauguration of President Carter, we have had a spate of reports about the monstrous waste of manpower the new administration discovered in the federal bureaucracy. People were sitting all week doing nothing in quiet corners on salaries of up to thirty thousand dollars a year. Discovered were armies of clerks and typists with absolutely nothing to do. One investigator said the main reason for all this was, contrary to private business practice, the pay of a government official depends solely on how many people he has under him. It makes no difference whether or not they do any work.

How seriously the situation has deteriorated in recent

years may be judged from one statistic. Our armed forces, which number about three million men and women, are reputed to have five times as many generals and admirals as during the peak period of World War II when we had ten million under arms and in uniform.

The take-it-easy philosophy obviously leads to a more tolerant attitude toward crime, which costs the nation a total of about $125 billion a year.

It is a universally accepted maxim that the greatest victory one can win in life is to triumph over one's self. Both as a nation and as individuals, that is the kind of victory Americans can win by restoring and maintaining the work ethic.

Every one of us must decide that living to work is right, after all, and that we will follow that path all our lives and teach our children to follow it.

12.

TIME TO STEM THE TIDE

Unless we return to the work ethic and reach a lasting solution to stagflation, the outlook for our children and grandchildren will be grim indeed.

We will leave them in a situation more hopeless than the defeated Confederate soldiers faced after Appomattox. They had to walk hundreds of miles through the ravaged southern countryside and begin picking up the threads of their lives under the guns of the occupying Union army.

They had their land. They could plant crops and feed themselves. They were men hardened in battle and their women had endured hardships at home. They were not demoralized, nor had they suffered any real loss of self esteem. But they were penniless and their farms were bereft of animals and tools.

It took the South seventy-five years to recover from the defeat in the Civil War. If we lose the battle against stagflation, there likely will be no recovery in the foreseeable future. The trends in America today can lead not only to economic ruin but to a total loss of self-esteem and ethical standards.

Books have been appearing recently advising people how to avoid the perils of "the coming deflation" and "the coming depression." The authors of some of these books are professionals in the business of selling market advisory letters. If those chaps know as much as they pretend about the economy and the stock market, why don't they just use their knowledge to get rich and not go through all the drudgery of preparing and selling market letters? They are cousins to the kind of racing experts who manage to pick a lot of winners by the simple expedient of touting each horse in every race to a different sucker.

We don't need to talk about a coming depression, we are in a depression now, but instead of the terrible deflation of the depression of the 1930s, we are having continued uncontrolled inflation. The press, particularly such prestigious dailies as the *Wall Street Journal* and *The New York Times*, reports that many business leaders fear early renewal of the high inflation rates of 1973 and 1974 as President Carter's spending to create jobs gets rolling. Things are not the same as they were in 1933 when President Franklin Roosevelt began his New Deal spending. We no longer have a huge gold reserve that can be doubled in official price to finance public works and other pump priming efforts. Nor are taxes low as they were in 1933. FDR was able to raise taxes sharply on top of doubling the gold price.

The other nations of the world were then in much worse economic and financial shape than we were. Even though FDR increased government expenditures beyond anything Americans ever had dreamed of before, absolutely no inflation of the dollar resulted either at home or abroad until World War II.

The depression we are in now is nowhere near as acute as the Hoover depression. That disaster bowled over nearly one-sixth of all the businesses in the country. Registered unemployment reached sixteen per cent as against seven per cent now. But this depression is bad enough and the prospect for rapid recovery is very poor.

The Hoover depression resulted from a long, slow deterioration of the basic economy during the 1920s. The dramatic collapse of the stock market in October, 1929, following many months of frantic speculation, was believed at the time to be the main cause. We now know that the stock market collapse was not enough to cause the terrible deflation and unemployment of the Hoover era.

The present depression, on the other hand, is clearly entirely the result of inflation, the energy shortage and the growing shortages of raw materials. Our taxes now are sky high and our federal deficit staggering. Some nations, notably West Germany, Switzerland and Sweden, are much better off financially than we are. Even Japan is better off in some respects.

FDR's spending eased, but did not end the 1930s

depression. President Carter has to spend money to keep people from starving or sinking into despair. It is naive folly to imagine that this spending will do more than treat the more obvious and painful symptoms of our present difficulties. Spending on essentially unproductive activities to make jobs won't cure anything.

So we must look for other ways both to end the current depression and to bring a permanent halt to uncontrolled inflation.

In our efforts to halt boondoggles, to prevent wasteful pipe dreams, and to halt further deterioration of the environment, we must beware of adopting an anti-technology posture that could lead to decay. Professor Jean Gimpel, a French scholar, wrote recently that the decision of the United States a few years back not to proceed with the development of a supersonic airliner marked a turning point in American history and a reversal of the previous enthusiasm of the American people for technological advance. Perhaps Professor Gimpel was mainly voicing French anger over the American government's long delay in granting landing rights at New York for the Anglo-French Concorde supersonic airliner. But his warning that we appear in European eyes to be turning our backs to renewed technological advance cannot be taken lightly.

If it is true that sustained uncontrolled inflation always is a reflex of war or the fear of war, then the first thing we must do is to end or vastly reduce the fear of war. This fear has weighed so heavily on the world for the past thirty years and has laid such a heavy burden on us to maintain the armed forces and the defense industry juggernaut that reduction of such fear cannot be accomplished without a very great change in our foreign policy.

We can take it for certain that Russia and the other communist nations are not going to abandon their belief that Marxism will ultimately rule the whole world. Many western scholars, and Russian dissidents like Andrei Amalrik, hope that the erosion of faith in Marxism will come first in Russia itself. In an essay written in 1969, Amalrik expressed doubt that Marxism could last another fifteen years in Russia. But we Americans cannot wait for that. We must maintain our moral, political and military strength at reasonable standards and at the same time strive earnestly and with united will to bring about a true and effective detente.

We must adapt our thinking to the realization that a great change has already occurred. It is not the fortuitous break between Moscow and Peking that we must adapt to as much as to the fact that the Soviet Union is no longer ruled by paranoids like Stalin and Beria, or by intractable boors like Molotov, Bulganin and Khrushchev. We must learn to distinguish between the sabre rattling propaganda put out by the Kremlin in *Pravda* and the TASS news agency and the sober thinking of the new breed of Russian intellectuals to whom Brezhnev and the Russian communist party's other top leaders undoubtedly listen. Here is an example of the new Soviet thinking—

Georgi Arbatov, director of the Institute of U.S. and

Canadian Studies of the USSR Academy of Sciences, said in an interview in *Der Spiegel* of Hamburg in February, 1977:

> According to Western figures, the Warsaw Pact nations have only 4.6 million troops opposed to NATO's 5.1 million. Our medium range missiles are opposed to 7,000 American nuclear warheads in Western Europe as well as the not inconsiderable might of Great Britain and France. Just imagine that the U.S. had on its northern border, instead of Canada, the Warsaw Pact nations and that, in the south, Mexico with a growing nuclear potential, was laying claim to one of its states, and that, instead of oceans to the east or west, there were Germans or Japanese. Then the U.S. would most likely develop a stronger conventional military capability.
>
> We have only two possibilities and our choice depends in large part on the West. Either we go the route of arms limitation and military parity or we tighten our belts and develop a defense force that will prevent a repetition of 1941.

Arbatov then was reminded that, unlike in 1941, neither side now has any intention of attacking the other. He replied "That is why we are optimistic. We prefer the first route. We would do anything to make it possible."

Answering another question, Arbatov said he did not believe there was any chance of U.S.-Soviet relations taking a turn for the worse. He said,

> There will be ups and downs but the basic policy of reaching an understanding will remain. There is no real alternative for either side. If Carter is serious about directing his attention to domestic social and economic problems, he must have a foreign policy that complements this objective. He has said he is for disarmament. And that is at the heart of detente.

Arbatov's message is loud and clear. He does not think Russia and the United States are on a collision course. If that's true, both sides can start reducing the terrible inflationary burden of huge armed forces and vast defense establishments. We should also consider the fact that the growing shortage of energy in the world makes it dubious that any nation will ever again be able to wage conventional war on a large scale.

We need to do much more, though, to stem the tide of disaster. For one thing, we must slash the burden of crime. More important than the direct cost of crime is the urgent need to revitalize the national conscience and reverse the moral destruction of our youth. We must tighten up the procedure in the juvenile courts and recognize that adolescents are not juveniles but are fully responsible for their offenses. Many people are muddleheaded and sentimental about this because of a lack of historical perspective. The notion that young people are not responsible for their actions until they are fully grown is a modern legal fiction that has no basis in scientific fact.

In the ancient world, a boy of eleven or twelve was considered a fully responsible adult. Kings' sons and brothers were considered able to sit on the royal council or to command armies in the field at the age of fourteen or fifteen. Edward VI ordered and supervised a complete revision of the services and canons of the Church of England when he was fifteen and the Prayer Book he thus created is still in use five hundred years later. The Vietcong army that defeated South Vietnam and held off U.S. regular troops for a decade was nearly half composed of boys, and some girls, under sixteen.

Under our present social system teenagers enjoy enormous freedom but are under precious little obligation to behave responsibly. They can and do commit thousands of vicious crimes and get away with them.

That must be stopped.

A little over half a century ago, some well-meaning people declared "There are no bad children, only bad parents." Two generations of Americans accepted this bit of asinine sentimentality and gradually a system of juvenile hocus pocus grew up that has undermined much of our whole system of law enforcement. A halt should have been called to this idiocy years ago; instead, the sentimentalists have had their way and things have gotten a lot worse. Kids are no longer content with shoplifting and other petty pilfering and vandalism. They now engage in muggings, rape and murder, usually with immunity.

The cumulative impact of this maudlin sentimentality about teenage crime causes undisciplined, irresponsible teenagers to grow up into irresponsible and corrupt adults. Such adults lack the moral stamina to resist the extreme pressures of our present combination of unrestrained inflation and depression. High as the cost of street crime and other violent offenses has risen, this cost is tiny as compared with the scores of billions of dollars we pay each year for unconscionable price gouging and corrupt rip-offs planned and executed by business and professional persons and the politicians.

I have given some rather abundant examples of this frightful inflationary toll in previous chapters. The ironic fact is that much of this corruption is perfectly legal. We are at present, a nation largely without individual consciences. Even our much touted new concern over civil rights, may be in large degree, only an attempt to avoid facing up to the consequences of our more elemental sins of greed and tolerance of corruption and violence.

If we don't bring an end to these outrages now, they will wreck the American economy and drag us down to the level of the most backward nations at no distant future.

One of the most alarming aspects of the situation is that, in spite of the basic mistake of Marxism, the communist bloc nations presently are doing a somewhat better job of reaching their economic goals than we are. They are still winning political and military victories in many parts of the world. We should not deceive ourselves with the comforting reflection that life in the communist countries is a lot harder in every respect than it is in the United States. What matters are the long term trends, not the present reality. The communists have managed to avoid uncontrolled inflation and we have not. In spite of some setbacks, communist technology has come a long way in the struggle to overcome the lead of the West and they have become globally dominant in some industries, ocean shipping example. Russia produces more steel than we do and is self-sufficient in energy while we are falling behind in the drive for self sufficiency.

This should not astonish us. Seventy years ago, Theodore Roosevelt, who had just completed mediating the 1905 Russo-Japanese war, declared that unless Russia "was destroyed by the unrest within her" she must "someday achieve a position of overshadowing power in the world." This is because she was the youngest of the great powers and had by far the most potential resources. Halford McKinder, the eminent British geographer, held the same view.

So, even if we no longer are on a military collision course with Russia, it will take a tremendous effort on our part to maintain a reasonable degree of economic and political equilibrium with her in the coming decades. We certainly cannot do so if we fail to put an end to uncontrolled inflation.

A major consequence of our failure to stay ahead of the communists politically and economically has been the loss of our position in Latin America along with the collapse of democratic republicanism throughout the entire region. Even the Filipinos, whom we liberated from Japanese conquest, have lost faith in us and have abandoned democracy. All of Latin America, except Mexico, is now under the rule of military dictatorships of the right or left. Mexico's new President Lopez Portillo told President Carter bluntly that he has no hope of solving Mexico's worsening problems without massive help from Washington—help we are in a very poor position to give. We can see in Lopez Portillo's entreaties the workings of Andrei Amalrik's remarks quoted in the last chapter on the crisis of world liberalism. People no longer believe they can stand alone and if we don't help them, they will resort to fascism or turn to the communists. The help they are asking for is not just money. They want political and moral understanding and sympathy as well as economic aid.

Closer to home is the prospect that uncontrolled inflation and failure to improve productivity might cause bankruptcy of our Social Security system and of most of the private pension funds by 1985. Already, a number of pension experts are predicting that long before the end of the century the principle of compulsory retirement at age sixty-five will have to be abandoned. This will occur because neither business nor government will be able to afford such a huge pension burden. That could be a good thing. Compulsory retirement is horribly frustrating to individuals, and the plain truth is that many workers and executives in their late sixties and early seventies are then at their peak productive capacity.

Bills already have been offered in the legislatures of several states. Bills are planned in Congress to outlaw compulsory retirement at age sixty-five without proof of diminished capacity. The experts who are predicting abandonment of compulsory retirement, say Social Security and other tax burdens on business will become so great by around 1990, that all private pensions may have to be abandoned.

Compulsory retirement came as an unforseen consequence of the adoption of the Social Security System. People took advantage of the opportunity to retire. Employers took advantage of the opportunity to get rid of higher paid older workers, substituting the cheaper labor of young workers hard up for jobs. In time, this began to backfire, particularly since the experience, knowledge and drive of the older worker ceased to be available. This fact alone, has had a tremendous effect on our nation's decline in productivity since World War

II. That is also a most powerful argument in favor of taking vigorous steps to reform the inflationary national tax structure described in Chapter 7.

Predictions that the Social Security system would become bankrupt and unable to meet the required payments to an expanding army of pensioners have been heard for some years. The figures cited are alarming, and the only certain ways of preventing disaster are to increase national productivity so more workers will be paying into the fund. There may be attempts to get more people to defer retirement so payments will be somewhat reduced.

The burden of military pensions is also becoming alarmingly inflationary. Defense Secretary Harold Brown said pensions to servicemen who retire very young, threaten to make personnel costs absorb 55 per cent of the entire defense budget. President Carter already has moved to restructure military pensions to eliminate "double dipping," the unique feature that allows military retirees to collect their full pensions while holding other government jobs. Rep. Les Aspin, D-Wisconsin, has introduced a bill he said will save the nation $80 billion on military pensions by the end of the century. Aspin's bill would allow members of the armed forces to retire as early as they do now, but they could not actually start collecting pensions until age fifty-five to sixty-two, depending on total length of active service.

Writing in the New York *Journal of Commerce*, Robert Lewin said in a series of articles in February 1977 that the Railroad Retirement Fund, which one million pensioners and other beneficiaries depend on as the chief source of their livelihoods, will be bankrupt by

1986 unless drastic steps are taken. He said the cold arithmetic admitted to no doubt about this and quoted the fund's chief actuary, Dr. Robert E. Larson of Chicago. The annual excess of payments to pensioners over receipts grew from $157 million in 1971 to $575 million in 1975. The railroad pensions range from $763 to more than $1,100 a month compared with Social Security pensions of $412 to $619 a month in the same brackets.

The actuaries are demanding that either taxes to support the fund be increased, or the pensions be slashed. Either course would lead to a political battle. The taxes already are heavy, 21.2 per cent of the first $1,375 of every worker's monthly pay. The carriers pay three quarters of the tax, the workers one quarter. The railroads pay an additional 12½ cents in supplemental benefits every hour each employee works.

Only one conclusion can be drawn from all these dismal facts. We cannot tolerate continued inflation at rates exceeding three per cent (it's running at five per cent at this writing) and we ought to be getting it down to 1.5 per cent.

No amount of sacrifice or hardship is too great to contemplate in order to achieve that goal. If we don't achieve it, the twilight of the most splendid civilization the world ever has seen will be at hand in a very few years. Americans can stand hardships and make sacrifices. We got through the Civil War, the Great Depression of the 1930s and World War II. World War I touched us comparatively lightly. We have survived the humiliation of political (but not military) defeat in Vietnam. But none of these disasters posed anywhere near as great a threat to the Union, or to all of us as individuals, as the present crisis of simultaneous economic stagnation and unrestrained inflation.

If we fail to win this struggle, the penalty will not be mere humiliation. Defeat will bring widespread poverty and a vast acceleration of the levels of corruption and crime. This in turn will drive a sufficient number of Americans into the kind of despair that breeds large outbreaks of violence and terror.

It is time to remember John F. Kennedy's ringing admonition: "Ask not what your country can do for you; ask what you can do for your country!"

In my five and a half decades of life I have developed an uncanny romance with these United States of America.

I have been increasingly concerned as I have matured, with the development of a three-pronged attack that has vitiated American social and economic progress:

—The TV tube has made us a nation of watchers instead of doers.

—The computer has eliminated much of the need to think; instead we push buttons.

—The credit card has made it too easy for us to become financial cripples, irresponsible and often bankrupt.

If the contents of this book accomplish anything at all, I hope my readers will recognize the pitfalls that I have outlined so that we can avoid a tremendous fall into disaster for our generation and our children.